YOU CAN'T
PREDICT A HERO

YOU CAN'T PREDICT A HERO

FROM WAR TO WALL STREET, LEADING IN TIMES OF *CRISIS*

JOSEPH J. GRANO, JR.

WITH MARK LEVINE

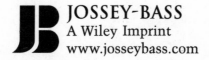

JOSSEY-BASS
A Wiley Imprint
www.josseybass.com

Published by Jossey-Bass
A Wiley Imprint
989 Market Street, San Francisco, CA 94103-1741—www.josseybass.com

Jossey-Bass books and products are available through most bookstores. To contact Jossey-Bass directly call our Customer Care Department within the U.S. at 800-956-7739, outside the U.S. at 317-572-3986, or fax 317-572-4002.

Jossey-Bass also publishes its books in a variety of electronic formats. Some content that appears in print may not be available in electronic books.

Library of Congress Cataloging-in-Publication Data

Grano, Joseph J. Jr., 1948-
     You can't predict a hero : from war to Wall Street, leading in times of crisis / Joseph J. Grano Jr., with Mark Levine. — 1st ed.
        p. cm.
     Includes index.
     ISBN 978-0-470-41167-4 (cloth)
     1. Grano, Joseph J. Jr., 1948- 2. Investment advisors—United States—Biography. 3. Executives—Psychology. 4. Leadership. 5. Executive ability.
I. Levine, Mark, 1958- II. Title.
HG4928.5.G72 2009
332.6092—dc22
     [B]   2009023240

Printed in the United States of America
FIRST EDITION
HB Printing   10 9 8 7 6 5 4 3 2

To the magnificent individuals whom I have had the honor to lead in the course of my military and business careers:

> *The dedicated warriors I guided on covert missions in the rain forests of Latin America*
>
> *The citizen soldiers I commanded on patrols through the jungles of Vietnam*
>
> *The wonderful men and women I led through the canyons of Wall Street*
>
> *My success is due in no small measure to their efforts.*
>
> *And to my lovely wife, Kathy, and my children, Angela, Andrea, and Joe, for their unstinting support and, most of all, their love*

CONTENTS

It is not the critic who counts; not the man who points out how the strong man stumbles, or where the doer of deeds could have done them better. The credit belongs to the man who is actually in the arena, whose face is marred by dust and sweat and blood; who strives valiantly; who errs, and comes up short again and again, because there is no effort without error and shortcoming; but who does actually strive to do the deeds; who knows the great enthusiasms, the great devotions; who spends himself in a worthy cause; who at the best knows in the end the triumph of high achievement, and who at the worst, if he fails, at least fails while daring greatly, so that his place shall never be with those cold and timid souls who know neither victory nor defeat.

—THEODORE ROOSEVELT

FOREWORD

By Lee Iacocca

I never thought I'd say this, but there are days when I despair of our country's future.

I'm 82 years old and I've seen what America can do. I've seen us overcome the Great Depression and emerge victorious in World War II. I've seen us send men to the moon and return them safely home again. From the private sector I've worked with governments to deal with the oil crisis of the 1970s and to turn around one of America's great companies. How did we do it? With leadership, both from the private sector and our elected leaders. And with an active, informed population, engaged and discerning about their personal and electoral choices.

In recent years, however, there's been a lack of leadership in business and politics, and a lack of involvement and wisdom among our citizens. Our government often seems run by incompetents, ideologues, and naysayers. Our corporations appear to be run largely by selfish elitists concerned more with the health of their own wallets than the health of their companies. And our fellow citizens look to be more concerned with appearance than substance.

Meanwhile, we're more dependent on foreign oil than ever, our deficits continue to soar, entitlement reform goes unaddressed, our health care crisis explodes, our trade deficit grows wider, our competitive edge in the marketplace vanishes, and our middle class—the great engine of national prosperity—slowly dies. That's why I asked, in my recent book, Where Have All the Leaders Gone?

Well, one of them can be found right here in the pages of this book. Joe Grano epitomizes what I call the nine Cs of leadership: curiosity, creativity, communication skills, character, courage, conviction, charisma, competence, and common sense.

His current work with Centurion Holdings shows his ongoing curiosity. His creativity is evident in the way he has always reached beyond the conventional wisdom to solve problems. Joe's communication skills are unparalleled, as anyone who has ever heard him speak can attest to. Everyone who has ever worked with him can attest to his character. As for courage, the scars he still bears are all the proof you need. His conviction has been clear every time he has stood up for doing what is right, regardless of the cost. Joe's charisma is obvious when you watch as he inspires college students in giant lecture halls and fellow CEOs around conference tables. As for competence, this is a man who turned around a troubled Wall Street firm in a year, and then set it on the right future course. And there's no one who brings a more common sense approach to problem solving than Joe, as you'll read in his suggestions for how we, as a nation, can address the current and looming crises we face.

Joe Grano is the kind of leader we sorely miss, both on Wall Street and in government. I share with him the hope that the story he tells in these pages helps inspire a new generation of national leaders to pick up the torch.

PREFACE

By its very nature, a book on leadership takes a myopic view of the world. Individual leadership is obviously crucial, particularly in a crisis. But it is never the only part of the story. A great leader can motivate employees to overcome adversity, inspire soldiers to brave fire and take a hill, or rouse a populace to make personal sacrifices for a greater common cause. Yet without the best efforts of those motivated employees, inspired soldiers, and aroused citizens, the crisis will turn into catastrophe.

Simply put, I'm a successful businessman who grew up working class and climbed the economic ladder on the strength of hard work, street smarts, leadership skills, and, to be immodest, character. While I am not a complete unknown, particularly among Wall Streeters, mine is certainly not a household name. The average man or woman on the street is not clamoring to hear what Joe Grano has to say.

Yet by virtue of when I was born and came of age in this country, I have served at the front lines of some of the major turning points in our nation's history—the crises, moments of harrowing struggle, and extraordinary success that our country and economy have gone through over the past forty years. While many books offer theories on leadership and ruminations on ideologies, I share with you the experience of what it means to lead at a time of crisis—when the stakes are human life, our country's freedom, people's life savings and livelihoods, and your own character. In the process, I hope that I help you become as good a business leader as you can be, enabling you to survive, and perhaps even thrive, in difficult circumstances.

My experience is hard won, and in many cases a baptism by fire, whether turning a demoralized rifle company into the most effective combat unit in Vietnam, piloting a venerable but declining Wall Street firm through stock market crashes to emerge more profitable than ever before, or helping my industry and my country weather the terrorist attacks of 9/11. I have led others through moments of great physical, psychological, and economic struggle, and through a unique vantage point, I have seen our world's leaders and what enables them to weather and triumph in times of crisis.

Leading others through both success and adversity can take an enormous personal toll in terms of health and relationships with loved ones, as I've witnessed personally. But with this belief in a greater good, a moral responsibility to do right by others, and a strength to make hard decisions and stick by them, anything is possible.

YOU CAN'T
PREDICT A HERO

"The leaders I most admire have never been those you see on the front pages or on the evening news but rather those I call the 'quiet heroes' who, far from the spotlights, motivate, teach, inspire, and that is … lead.

Joe Grano has done that—in war, in the boardroom, and with his family and friends. He tells his story as a great leader should—humbly, and with an eye to teaching readers how they can benefit from his experiences."

—GEORGE PATAKI, FORMER GOVERNOR OF NEW YORK

Chapter One

LEADERS: ARE THEY BORN OR MADE?

Leadership is the ability to gain the willing support of subordinates. Any manager can mandate certain actions by his or her employees, but only when an employee actually wants to support the mandate does the manager become a true leader. Great leaders earn this support seemingly without effort. When such an individual walks into a room, makes a speech, or is interviewed by the media, his or her personality traits are evident, if not always easily definable. A great leader's natural charisma instills confidence and creates a desire in others who experience it to want to follow.

I learned from an early age that others looked to me as a leader. This helped me grow from a Hartford, Connecticut, street kid to a captain in the Green Berets by the age of twenty-two. It contributed to my climb from stock broker trainee to a top management position at Merrill Lynch after returning from Vietnam with a 60 percent disability from severe wounds and no job prospects. Being able to leverage that charisma as a significant leadership tool was one of the reasons I was hired by

PaineWebber as president of retail sales and marketing and in one year turned a division that had lost $96 million into one that made profits of $13 million. When I took the helm as chairman and CEO of PaineWebber and steered it through an $11 billion merger with Swiss banking giant UBS, I relied heavily on my ability to motivate my subordinates. And during the national crisis of September 11, 2001, the subsequent anthrax attacks, and a stint as chairman of the President's Homeland Security Advisory Council, I called on all the leadership techniques I'd learned over the years.

In each of these roles, I have found four distinct functions of management that contribute to being able to lead and operate an organization, whether it is an infantry squad of twelve young men or a multibillion-dollar firm with thousands of employees. I use an acronym for these functions: PLOC, which stands for planning, leading, organizing, and controlling. Three of these four functions—planning, organizing, and controlling—can be delegated or supplemented to some degree. Of course, there is only so much responsibility you can turn over to others. Delegate too much and you could end up like Kenneth Lay, with a chief financial officer whose actions could possibly put you in prison. The one management function you cannot delegate at all is leadership.

Since it's the one function a manager can't delegate to associates, having the ability to lead is a requirement for success. So how does one come by this vital ingredient? After a speech I'd given to graduate students at the Amos Tuck School of Business Administration at Dartmouth College, I was asked the proverbial question supposed to unlock the mystery of leadership: Are leaders born, or are they made?

Obviously leadership skills and techniques can be acquired through education, whether it comes from formal schooling or experience. Business schools have made it a standard part of their curricula, and I received extraordinary formal leadership training from the U.S. Army. Leadership abilities can also come from observing the actions of other leaders and their experience. There are few things more educational than being placed in a situation where you have to take the lead. That's true if you're a young person playing sports after school or a mature adult leading a project group at the office. So leaders, to a degree, can be made.

Just as clearly, however, some are born to leadership. Charisma is evident at an early age, and an astute observer can pick out future leaders on a crowded playground. The magnetic pull of this genetic gift is evident in every field. Political leaders as diverse as Churchill and Gandhi displayed it. Religious leaders from Pope John Paul II to the fourteenth Dalai Lama, exhibited it. Military leaders from Robert E. Lee to George S. Patton demonstrated it. And business leaders exemplify the trait just as clearly.

When a Jack Welch, Lee Iacocca, Richard Grasso, or Dan Tully emerges, there is no doubt that the intangible, unique leadership qualities they exemplify are part of their God-given DNA. The management savvy and leadership of Welch, who served as the chairman and CEO of General Electric from 1981 to 2001, is legendary. Iacocca solidified his place in the annals of business leadership for his crisis leadership while chairman and CEO of Chrysler from 1979 through 1992, rescuing the automaker from financial ruin. Grasso is another brilliant crisis leader. Joining the New York Stock Exchange as a clerk in 1968, he eventually rose to become chairman and CEO, solidifying the exchange's place as the most important stock market in the world and leading it back from the trauma of September 11, 2001. Tully may not be as well known as Welch, Iacocca, or Grasso, but he is every bit their equal in leadership genius. In his four years at the helm of Merrill Lynch, Tully steered the firm to record earnings and completed its shift from a retail brokerage to a global investment banking power.

I grew up in a working-class neighborhood in Hartford, Connecticut, called "The Avenue." It's a ten- to twenty-square block roughly triangular neighborhood bordered by Franklin, Wethersfield, Maple, and Fairfield avenues. There were lots of other Italian Americans there, but the 'hood also included Jews, Hispanics, and African Americans, and for most of us, our grandparents or parents were immigrants.

My earliest memories are of living on the third floor of my grandparents' huge four-family home at 218 Franklin Avenue. I still have no idea how they were able to afford that house. They certainly needed a big house since they had eleven children, each of whom lived in the house with their spouse and children when they were first married.

Hard times during the Great Depression led my father, Joseph, the oldest son, to enlist in the army to have a job. He was fifteen years old. Despite his age, he made a good soldier, serving nine years. He saw combat as an artilleryman in New Guinea in World War II and rose to the rank of master sergeant. When he came home from war, he was amazed that little Joan Phelps, who'd hung around with his younger siblings, had become a beautiful young woman. The attraction was obviously mutual because they soon married even though she was only sixteen. I was born a year later, in 1948, the first of their six sons.

My father had an entrepreneurial streak, but none of his businesses lasted long, and he'd end up back managing a construction crew. He never spoke about his business failures, but then he never spoke of any of his feelings. He would rather spend his time solving a problem than talking about it. He also had a temper, another trait I share.

My mother didn't have a temper. In fact, she didn't have a judgmental bone in her body. She cared about people for who they were rather than some notion of what anyone else thought they should be. She always worked outside the home, as either a waitress or on the third shift at some factory. But she made sure that on the weekends, our house was filled with extended family and friends. My mother had a magic touch with small children, and she entertained them with stories she made up. Each one had a moral, usually teaching a lesson of respect for others, such as a tale of a little boy who was continually teased for being short. Of course, at the end of the story, the little boy's lack of height allowed him to save the day for all the taller kids. All the children in our family, for three generations, came to know and love my mother's stories. One year, as a gift, I had them bound into a book and printed, making sure to include a family favorite, "Field of Dreams," about a lonely little girl who communicated with nature. My mother's easy rapport with children and adults alike taught me the value of embracing humanity.

My father was the hardest-working man I have ever known. He put in eighty hours a week on construction sites in order to feed and keep a roof over his wife and six sons. Due to both my parents' hard work, we were always well fed, but there was little money left for luxuries. And like most other youngsters, I craved some of those luxuries. So I learned that if I wanted a stylish new jacket to wear when I went out Saturday nights, I needed to earn the money myself. Emulating my father, I threw myself into work. At one time, I had two shoeshine boxes and two paper routes. I picked tobacco for two summers at fifty cents an hour. Today when I see a busboy clearing tables, I see myself in my mind's eye forty-five years ago.

The neighborhood kids divided up into gangs that we called "fraternities." These groups were defined not by ethnicity but by social style and status: there were the jocks, the greasers, the nerds, and the cool kids. Fights broke out every weekend among the different cliques, but if any group from outside the 'hood caused a problem, we all banded together.

Everyone in the neighborhood had a nickname; mine was Joey the Czar. I was a tough kid, and that helped me become a leader in my tough neighborhood. But I was also a hard worker, an A student, a stylish dresser, and a good dancer, all of which helped me become popular. That popularity boosted my confidence even more. As the oldest child of two working parents, I naturally took charge and was responsible from a very early age. I also showed respect to everyone—just as my parents did—and as a result, I received respect from everyone. The other kids, whatever their clique, came to me for advice and help. Throughout school, I was always elected class president, mostly because I was the only one receiving votes from individuals from across the various groups.

Knowing where I have come from, but also how much I'd learned about leadership techniques and tactics in the years since I'd left The Avenue, I told my questioner at Dartmouth that leaders are both born and made. I explained that there is a difference between great leaders and good leaders. Good managers can learn leadership skills and become good leaders. Great leaders, however, are born, not made. They naturally possess several indisputable qualities that define them:

- They care about people.
- They are optimistic by nature.
- They are generally good communicators.
- They have a natural charisma.
- They have a winning attitude and philosophy.
- They are decisive.
- They are good managers.
- They have vision.
- They are, to some degree, manipulative and selfish.
- They seek psychic income as much as, if not more than, real income.

When great leaders turn an organization into a winner, when they positively influence the careers and lives of tens of thousands of employees, or when they help a family or an individual deal with a crisis, they feel a shot of adrenaline from making a difference. But it's more than just something that makes them feel good: it defines their character. Great leaders are better givers than receivers because giving allows them to demonstrate and exercise their character to others as well as to themselves in ways that receiving does not.

Historians often note that it takes great crises to produce great leaders. I do not believe it is either coincidental or a sign of divine providence that the three presidents usually cited as our greatest leaders were in office during the three greatest crisis periods in our nation's history: George Washington, Abraham Lincoln, and Franklin Delano Roosevelt. I have always felt there are defining moments when clouds and chaos darken the sky, and friends, employees, or peers look for someone to provide solutions rather than postmortems. How a person, whether a combat leader, an executive, a parent, or a friend, responds to these challenges helps define his or her character. The opportunity afforded by a crisis provides a stage on which great leaders can reach their full potential.

All of these insights remained just an interesting intellectual exercise for me until I faced a personal triggering moment: my son was graduating from high school and heading off to Yale.

Joseph is the youngest of my three children and my only son, and I wanted to give him a meaningful and memorable gift. I knew no material object, whatever the cost, would fit the bill. I recognized that with my son leaving the roost, I was running out of time to compensate for all the years of seventy-hour workweeks and all the evenings and weekends spent at charitable events. He was going away to college, starting a new, more independent stage in his life and in our relationship, and what did he really know about me?

I have never been one to fully share my feelings and thoughts with my family. That might surprise people who know me through business and probably think of me as a typical outgoing, emotive Italian guy. I know stoicism is not politically correct these days, but I always admired my father's quiet strength. Because I am my father's son in many ways, most of what my own son knew about me didn't come from heart-to-heart father-son talks but from hearing some army buddy tell an embellished war story or listening to a business colleague deliver an overstated introduction at a testimonial dinner. I thought that for his high school graduation I should give my son something I had never offered him before: insights into who I really am, where I came from, and how I feel about not just him but family, work, education, life, friendship, marriage, money, politics, and everything else. I wanted to give him something I had unintentionally withheld from him and that had unintentionally been withheld from me as a young man: a chance to get emotionally close to his father.

I have always hand written letters to my direct reports throughout my corporate career. Sometimes these were brief notes at Christmas explaining why I had selected a particular gift for them. Other times these letters were lengthier and more detailed monologues, like when I wrote my good-byes and advice to my two dear friends who were succeeding me at UBS PaineWebber when I left. I have always felt that even someone as comfortable speaking off the cuff as I am can convey greater emotional and intellectual depth in letters than in telephone calls. I decided I would write a letter to my son.

Once I had committed to the idea, I spent hours each night writing notes and ideas in pencil on a legal pad. I started with my earliest memories, working chronologically. I began each writing session by going back over what I had written the day before, looking for gaps, omissions, and things I should clarify or expand. I promised myself I would tell the whole story, warts and all. When the story finally reached the present, I put together as a conclusion a list of all the advice I wanted to pass on to my son, from the mundane (always tip service providers at least 20 percent) to the profound (everyone, regardless of his or her job or position, is an equally valuable human being who deserves to be treated with respect).

When I finished revising this letter to my son, I rewrote it, again by hand, in a nicely bound journal, and presented it to him the day he graduated from high school. He took the journal into his room that evening and read it straight through. When he finished, he came out with tears in his eyes that brought tears to my eyes. He told me it was the best gift he had ever received.

Some of my tears were from the joy of connection to my son. But some were from regret. As you will read in the following pages, I believe all successful, ambitious people are selfish to some degree. You cannot set self-focused priorities and work the long hours that success demands without stealing time and energy from your relationships with loved ones. And you cannot assume they will be as satisfied with your achievements or the money you have earned as you are. Those are your goals, not your family's. I know my children paid a price for my success. The letter I wrote to my son was one attempt to repay that debt. Today I regret I didn't write similar letters to my two daughters when they graduated from high school and went off to college.

Writing that letter to my son also rekindled a calling that had lain dormant. My earliest career goal was to be a teacher, and throughout the careers I pursued, I always earned a special reward from mentoring young people. During my years at Merrill Lynch and UBS PaineWebber, this had been an informal process. I'd give commencement and other speeches at colleges and thoroughly enjoy the chance to engage with the next generation. I'd meet a young person by design or default, discern a spark that needed only encouragement to fully ignite, and offer him or her guidance and help. That letter to my son led me to create a formal mentoring program at my new consultancy, Centurion Holdings. I've brought in dozens of interns over the years and, often to the consternation of my staff, have devoted long hours to them. It was working with these young people that led me to write this book. I wanted to memorialize the best practices of leadership I'd learned and practiced and pass them on to those who will take up the mantle in the future.

I will tell you how I rehabilitated a company of scared and demoralized draftees after they lost twenty-seven of their comrades on an infamous hill in Vietnam. I will explain how I piloted a venerable but declining Wall Street firm through stock market crashes to emerge more profitable than ever before. I will write about how I helped my industry and my country weather the terrorist attacks of 9/11.

I hope my story will help you make the most of your own unique leadership gifts. By reviewing my own experiences and extrapolating from them a number of best practices, I can provide much of the knowledge needed to turn a good manager into a good leader. I hope my story can help a young person just starting out in business become an effective leader of a project team confronting a problem, teach a midlevel executive how best to confront an emergency in a department or division, or inspire a corporate executive to steer an organization in a crisis. And I hope that reading about how I addressed crises and adversity may awaken the dormant leadership spirit in young people like my son and my interns who may have hidden within them the potential to be our nation's next generation of great leaders.

My one hesitation about writing a book was that it would seem a self-serving vanity project. I have been an instinctive leader my entire life. Although I certainly learned lessons from my parents, my military commanders, and my business mentors, my leadership style developed ad hoc. For much, if not most, of my life, I led from my gut. As I matured and climbed the corporate ladder to the corner office, my leadership became more premeditated and manipulative. There's nothing wrong with a leader using spin, exaggeration, or even manipulation, I believe, as long as it's being done for the right reasons and the end result has a positive impact on all of an organization's constituencies. For me to explain my leadership practices and pass them on to you, I cannot cite treatises, studies, or scholarly texts. All I have to point to for examples are the things I have actually done as a leader in times of crisis. Therefore, I ask your indulgence in the pages that follow for any stories that appear self-aggrandizing.

Similarly, I ask the indulgence of those with whom I grew up, went to war, and have worked. The anecdotes and stories I tell in this book are based on my own recollections. However, I've never been a diarist, and I have lived my life at a pace that provides little time for introspection or meditation. As you'll read, I am neither a second-guesser nor an obsessive conductor of postmortems. Yes, I look for lessons learned, but my energy is always directed toward finding solutions and moving forward. If in the recounting of incidents in my past I have given short shrift to the roles and efforts of others, or have mischaracterized anyone's behavior, please accept my apologies. War stories, whether about actual combat or business battles, are not unlike fishing or golf stories. Sometimes things become more dramatic in the retelling. I have tried my best to avoid such embellishment. But if any has inadvertently slipped in, I hope you will chalk it up to the fading memory of a soldier rather than the pomposity of a corporate executive.

SIX PRECEPTS OF LEADERSHIP

Reviewing my life and careers in the military and the corporate world, and recounting the crises I've faced and overcome, has led me to identify six recurring leadership precepts.

1. PROBLEMS REQUIRE SOLUTIONS

Successful leaders position themselves as an extension of the solution rather than just the articulation of the problem. In times of crisis, pragmatism has to take priority over anger, politics, and personality. A common reaction to a crisis is to look for someone or something to blame. Although postmortems are important to ensure mistakes aren't repeated, it's vital to focus initially on how best to solve the problem. Scapegoats can often turn into saviors.

2. BE THE ETERNAL OPTIMIST

Being positive, optimistic, and focused on "can" rather than "can't" leads to a winning perspective that permeates an organization and can make the difference between failure and success.

3. RECONCILE YOURSELF TO SELFISHNESS

One key to leadership is reconciling yourself to your own selfishness. High achievers are inherently selfish to some extent: the time and energy demands required will force you to steal time from your family and friends. Similarly, in times of crisis, you need to factor in the centrality of self-interest to all your partners: clients, shareholders, and employees. This is a natural human trait, and leaders can often use it to move organizations in the desired direction, while sometimes it needs to be fought against.

4. YOU CAN'T PREDICT A HERO

It's impossible to predict how individuals will react when they're facing a crisis or dire circumstances. That's just as true for people facing financial bullets as real bullets. Those who are vociferously aggressive and demonstrative prior to a crisis can vanish when things get difficult. And the peers or subordinates you always thought most loyal and supportive might be the quickest to flee what they perceive to be a sinking ship or perhaps even stab you in the back.

5. THE TRUTH IS NEVER WRONG

Facts are stubborn. As much as you might like to have more time or wish for greater resources, to succeed in a crisis requires accepting the reality of a situation and working within its parameters. The truth is never wrong. You can't let enthusiasm, determination, or even patriotism stand between you and reality. Success doesn't come through hoping for long-shot, best-case scenarios to come true. It comes from asking questions, using whatever time is available to deliberate, and then taking action.

6. HUMANITY IS MORE IMPORTANT THAN HIERARCHY

The irreplaceable element of a good leader is that he or she cares about people. To lead effectively, you need to keep hierarchy separate from humanity. Positions and titles merit respect, regardless of who occupies or holds them. But so do individuals, regardless of what position they hold or title they have. You need to remember that your assets ride up and down the elevators. Efficient use of human assets is vital for overcoming crises.

I'd be remiss if I didn't add a cautionary note before I get much further in my discussion of leadership. Whether it sprang from my eternal optimism, my Green Beret training, or both, for most of my career I have believed that I could win the hearts and minds of anyone and everyone. It took me years to learn I was wrong. Even when you have cultivated a winning culture and built an effective team, there will remain a handful of naysayers and a small number of goldbricks who refuse to pull their weight. Remember that leadership is gaining the *willing* support of your subordinates. There will always be a few who refuse to be led no matter how dire the straits and how dynamic the leadership. That is why every leader needs to adopt as an attitude a quote I once read: "No passengers, no prisoners." When, despite all your efforts, a few holdouts don't contribute to the shared effort, let them go. No passengers! And when a splinter group continues to focus on the negative and doesn't want to be part of the team, let them go as well. No prisoners!

With that caveat duly noted, the following chapters explain and expand on the six precepts I've outlined drawing on my experiences. In the process, I hope that I help you fulfill your potential as a business leader.

I have one other secret hope for this book: that some of you who have stolen time from your spouses to further your careers, who are spending most of your hours of consciousness focused on your division rather than your children, who have never revealed your emotions to your family, will be inspired to write your own letters for your own loved ones.

I know those are some pretty big goals to set, but I've always aimed high.

"1LT Joseph Grano as an Operational Detachment "A" Commander has accomplished his mission in a truly outstanding manner through his consistent application of superior job knowledge and leadership capabilities. . . . 1LT Grano continually shows a very refreshing enthusiasm for his work, and this is exemplified in the initiative he takes, no matter what the task is. This drive combined with his above average intelligence, maturity and proven leadership abilities make him the most outstanding officer the undersigned has rated to date."
—CAPTAIN ANTHONY A. ABBOT, APRIL 1970

"This outstanding young officer seeks self improvement, to include sponsoring Latin American offices to increase his Spanish language capability. CPT Grano was constantly assigned to high priority projects which required initiative, motivation and devotion to duty. He accomplished every task in an outstanding manner and established the highest possible rapport with Latin American personnel."
—MAJOR CHARLES H. MCLENDON, SEPTEMBER 1970

"CPT Grano took the weakest rifle company within the battalion and has, in a short period of time, developed it into the strongest. His company was consistently the most successful of all companies when engaged in combat operations. Based not only on combat results but also on overall performance, his company was twice chosen as Battalion Honor Company. In my opinion CPT Grano could perform outstandingly in any assignment afforded him."
—MAJOR EDWIN S. MITTS JR., JUNE 1971

"I have observed CPT Grano as a battalion S-1 and S-4 and as a rifle company commander. Whatever the job he tackles it with enthusiasm and good judgement and accomplishes it in an outstanding manner. As a company commander he had the knack to inspire as well as the ability to make good tactical decisions. Consequently his company normally led the Brigade in destroying the enemy. His abilities are not confined to the battlefield. His company also scored high in command maintenance and evaluation inspections. He is a distinct asset to the Army and should be integrated into the Regular structure."
—COLONEL CHARLES R. SMITH, JUNE 1971

Chapter Two

PROBLEMS REQUIRE SOLUTIONS

Effective leaders focus on solutions, not scapegoats. Throughout my life, whenever a problem or a challenge confronted me, I have been able to set aside anger, frustration, and basic human desire to assign blame, and instead focus first and foremost on finding or creating a solution. Too often I have witnessed military officers, corporate executives, and politicians focused more on conducting a postmortem than on solving a problem or challenge. I have been through many crisis situations in which the senior person in the room began by asking, "Who did it?" This approach—accusing, blaming, and ultimately punishing—typically drives almost everyone else in the room into hiding. Ironically, the person responsible for a mistake is more often than not the one essential to rectify the situation. In a crisis, pragmatism has to take priority over anger, politics, and personality. Postmortems can be conducted only after you have stabilized the situation, and in order to avoid the same mistakes in the future. And anger and frustration can be vented only when they will not disrupt or even deter the process.

In the moment, however, a leader who is facing a situation that demands immediate attention must look for a solution. Clarity of focus and effort is one of the characteristics that sets effective leaders apart from typical executives and managers. Being trained in a problem-solving approach helps turn that approach to crises into a reflex. And the severity of the problems you face goes a long way toward sharpening your focus. I had the luck, both bad and good, to be well trained in problem solving by the U.S. Army and to face, repeatedly, that most severe of circumstances: combat.

After I graduated from high school, I was certain I would go on to college. I had the grades and the support of my family. As one of the third generation of Granos in America, I was expected to make the jump from the blue-collar working class to the white-collar middle class. I didn't realize it then, but I do now, that my generation was the fulfillment of my grandparents' and parents' American dream. Because I was good with numbers, had exceptional grades, and demonstrated a proven ability to lead, I decided I'd become a math teacher. It seemed a pragmatic choice, and considering my origins, it was a likely next step up the socioeconomic ladder. I entered Central Connecticut State University and moved into an apartment off campus with a bunch of other guys. I found the course work easy, and I ended up spending most of my time partying. One evening a bunch of us were sitting around playing cards. As the game went on into the late night and then early morning and the liquor continued to flow, we all started talking about Vietnam.

It was 1967, and the war had overwhelming public support. The United States was protecting a fledgling democracy against aggressive communist expansion in Southeast Asia as we had done in Korea in the 1950s. It was a given that my friends and I would all serve when we were drafted. Coming from very patriotic families, many of which had come to the United States only one or two generations before in pursuit of the American dream, we saw military service not as a sacrifice but as a duty. It was an expected rite of passage. My younger brother Nicky had already enlisted in the army and was serving with the 101st Airborne.

At about three o'clock in the morning as the card game wound down, I announced that rather than continue wasting time and money not studying in college, we should go and enlist now and finish college when we returned. Later that morning, three of us dragged our severely hung-over selves to the enlistment center in downtown Hartford. I was sworn in as a recruit to the U.S. Army.

As part of training at Fort Jackson in South Carolina, all the recruits were required to take an IQ test. I didn't think anything of it until a few weeks after, when I was ordered to meet with a delegation that had arrived from the Pentagon. The head of the delegation told me I'd earned the highest test score in the army and asked if I'd like to go to Officer Candidates School (OCS). He said the Pentagon was willing to waive the requirement of a college degree, since the army was eager for officers at that time. The only hitch was I'd need to change the terms of my enlistment from two years to three. I knew this was a real opportunity for a working-class kid and agreed to extend my commitment. When my father, the former master sergeant, saw the gold second lieutenant bars on my shoulders, he looked at me with a new-found respect.

I loved OCS. I worked my ass off and decided I wanted to become a Green Beret, a member of the U.S. Army Special Forces. (Created in the early 1960s at the urging of President Kennedy, Special Forces work with and within the local populations of areas of interest to the United States.) I submitted my request and was the only graduate to receive orders to report for assignment to Special Forces training. Unfortunately the brigade commander didn't want to let me go. I earned a high profile within my OCS class, which brought me to the attention of the brigade commander. He decided that I should impart my leadership skills to subsequent officer candidates, and he ultimately convinced the Pentagon to reassign me to his brigade as a training officer. I was so angry that I put my fist through a latrine door. But my experience in the army up until that point, while brief, had taught me the best way to overcome this kind of bureaucratic problem would be to keep on excelling and prove myself. Protesting would get me nowhere quickly, whereas if I demonstrated skill as a trainer, I would be even more attractive to Special Forces, whose primary role was teaching counterinsurgency to indigenous personnel.

I served my time as a training officer and received outstanding evaluations. Once again I applied for assignment with Special Forces and was accepted. This time the brigade commander couldn't stand in my way. The only catch was that I needed to again extend my military commitment, this time for another two years. I didn't think twice: the idea of being a Green Beret appealed to me on many levels. It was a chance for me, a working-class kid from Hartford, to join the nation's elite, train with the best of the best, serve my country in the kind of overt way that most appealed to a young patriot's idealism, and lead. Six years of my life then seemed like little price to pay.

Special Forces training was rigorous. In addition to studying insurgency, counterinsurgency, and civic action, I was sent to jump and SCUBA schools. Because Green Berets must be bilingual, I spent six months in language school studying Spanish. I came in number one in my language class and, not coincidentally, received orders to report to the Eighth Special Forces Group, headquartered in Colón, Panama.

Green Berets are trained to function independently in small groups, called A Teams, train indigenous personnel, and lead them in operations. We would be given a mission, shown a problem, and told to come up with a solution as quickly and efficiently as possible. Once we had the mission, we were sequestered in a room to study the numerous variables that could influence its success. This preparatory phase was called *isolation*. The A team would remain in isolation until the moment we left for the mission. We studied the terrain, targets, and idiosyncrasies of the language. A Spanish word or phrase heard in Peru could mean something totally different in, say, Mexico. Our missions varied but in general focused on one of three activities: training a country's armed forces to combat insurgents, training insurgents to combat the regime in power, or conducting civic action, such as building a school in remote areas to assist the populace. It was a given that we'd always be outnumbered and would be serving either on the front line or behind enemy lines.

My team's principal area of geographical responsibility was Central America and Cuba, although every A team in the

Eighth Special Forces Group could be assigned at any time to any country in Latin America. We were prepared to become "sterile" in hostile areas: that meant we'd remove all the name tags from our uniforms, take off our dog tags, and sign statements that if we were captured, we would deny our status and be categorized as mercenaries.

My time in Latin America was an unbelievable experience. I was a twenty-year-old Green Beret first lieutenant commanding a twelve-man A team made up of highly skilled, incredibly motivated noncommissioned officers. Each team member was trained not only in his own specialty—weapons, communications, medical, or intelligence, for example—but also cross-trained in all the other specialties. Every man was a volunteer who was superb at his job. The camaraderie was extraordinary. It allowed me to lead a small, highly motivated team, facing incredible odds, and succeed. That accomplishment strengthened my sense of purpose and self-confidence.

As a Green Beret, I got to do all sorts of things no kid from Hartford could have ever dreamed of. For all the danger and pressure, or maybe because of it, we had more than our fair share of fun. One early training mission brought both laughter and excitement—the laughter came at my expense, and all in all it was quite a humbling experience.

Immediately after arriving, my A team was assigned to the Apollo Recovery Team. If the capsule came down on land anywhere south of Mexico, our job was to get to the site and secure it. Because of that, we had to be trained to parachute into triple-canopy jungle terrain.

Triple canopy jungle can exceed a hundred feet in depth of very thick jungle, and parachuting into such dense and deep jungle is perilous because your body can ricochet off trees. A broken neck was not out of the question. In addition, you could more than likely find yourself hanging eighty feet off the ground as your parachute entangled with the hundred-foot-dense jungle. We chose to employ a body suit used by smoke jumpers who parachuted into the woods to combat forest fires. The suits were made of heavy canvas and had straps protecting your underarms and crotch from tree limbs.

On the day designated to practice jumping into triple-canopy jungle with our smoke jumper suits, the group command changed our exercise from landing in the thick jungle to simply landing on a traditional drop zone, a field approximately ten acres in size. The group command had decided at the last moment they did not want to sacrifice the parachutes for a training exercise. The drop zone looked like a postage stamp on a surrounding jungle envelope.

Each member of my A team used steerable parachutes. These parachutes look like any other except for an eight-foot hole in the back part of the parachute canopy that allows the jumper to alter the maneuverability of the chute. After you jumped from the plane and your parachute deployed, you pulled out a pin on your left and right harnesses to steer the parachute into or against the wind. This allowed you to also speed up or slow down the descent and direct the flight. Prior to every jump into the tiny landing zone, each member donated five dollars into a pool. The team member who landed closest to the center of the landing zone won the pool.

I always ensured that, as commander, I was the first to enter and the last to leave an area of operations, so I was the first one to jump out of the plane on our training exercise.

After jumping, I found myself in a deep cloud. I couldn't see a thing and waited to pull the pins that would allow me to steer my parachute. When I finally cleared the cloud, I was only three hundred feet from the ground and directly over the French Canal, which had as frequent residents barracudas and crocodiles. In the distance, I could see the remainder of my A team approaching the designated landing zone. My choices were limited: take a swim in the French Canal or pull my pins and head for the triple-canopy jungle. I chose the latter.

My body bounced and ricocheted through the trees, and sure enough, I found myself hanging eighty feet from the ground. According to the original training plan, I removed my repelling rope, anchored it within the parachute's harness, and repelled down to the ground. Fifteen minutes later, a lieutenant colonel in a jeep arrived and asked, "Lieutenant, do you know you have an eight-foot hole in the back of your parachute?"

"Yes sir," I responded.

"Well, use it next time, son," he advised.

No one else had been caught in the low-hanging cloud, and because of that, I achieved something never to be equaled in the history of the Eighth Special Forces Group: I was the only A team commander ever to have landed on the other side of the French Canal. Where I landed was named "Grano's LZ," as I found out the next day when I received a standing ovation at the group's picnic. Not a bad introduction for the group's new commander of an A team, the Apollo Recovery Team, and the parachute school. I can just imagine how well my pink face resonated with my Green Beret uniform as a backdrop.

Although there were lots of adventures and cloak-and-dagger stuff, most of what we did was train others. My A team ran a jump school that taught most of the elite Latin American military forces. We'd spend months at a time working with the officers and men from allied nations. Ironically, I was teaching, just as I planned to do after college, albeit teaching airborne and counterinsurgency operations rather than algebra and trigonometry.

The entire time I was in Panama, I knew that eventually I'd be going to Vietnam. It wasn't a question of if, but when. I was now thinking of a career in the military, and the kind of combat I was experiencing in Latin America wasn't the kind that made it into official military reports. When you're young, highly trained, and superpatriotic, you want to go into combat; you want to put all the leadership and tactical skills you've acquired to the supreme test. I looked forward to getting orders sending me to Southeast Asia, and one day I got my wish. Before going, however, I had one more thing to do: get married.

While in Panama, I'd met a beautiful Peruvian dancer named Carmen. Demonstrating the spontaneity and impulsiveness that have always been common among young soldiers and women during wartime, we decided to get married as soon as I received my orders to report to Vietnam. I dropped my wife, who spoke no English and who, we soon learned, was pregnant, at my parents' house in Hartford and boarded a plane to Vietnam.

In 1971 I arrived at the headquarters of the 198th Infantry Brigade in Duc Pho, a village in Quang Tri Province right by the former demilitarized zone that separated North and South Vietnam. I went directly to see the major serving as the brigade's staff officer in charge of personnel, referred to as the G1. After going over my records and seeing I'd just come from serving as commander of a Green Beret A team in Central America, he said he had the perfect job for me: command of the brigade's Ranger Battalion. That was just the kind of assignment I'd wanted: leading a crack unit of highly motivated volunteers. Most battalion commanders are lieutenant colonels, so it was quite a compliment for a junior captain. But just then the telephone rang.

There was a short, intense conversation. "Yes, sir, I've got one right here," the major said to the person calling him, while looking right at me. When he hung up the phone, he said to me, "Well, Captain, things have changed." That call had come from the brigade's maneuver commander who was in an orbiting chopper. Company A was pinned down on top of a hill called the Rock Pile and was taking heavy casualties. The general had just relieved the company commander and needed someone to get those boys off the hill. I was it. So instead of leading an elite battalion of volunteers, I'd be taking charge of a straight leg, regular infantry company of demoralized draftees. Of the approximately 130 men in Company A, 27 were already fatalities. The men on the ground were left without a company commander, and morale was suffering, if not on the verge of collapse. My job would not be easy.

The Rock Pile is one of a series of prominent rocky outcroppings not far from Khe Sanh, which would remain the site of heavy fighting for both the Army and Marine Corps throughout the entire Vietnam War. Company A was stuck on the hill, its positions zeroed in on by North Vietnamese Army (NVA) machine guns and mortar fire. Every transport chopper that had tried to get through a well-designated cross fire had been badly shot up.

The damage to Company A had already occurred prior to my landing in Khe Sanh, which was the battalion rear. Those heroic soldiers had already gone through hell. I needed to assess the situation and asked for a helicopter to observe the area. I requested a Huey gunship to fly me to the Rock Pile.

The chopper pilots weren't eager to take on the mission. "No way," one said, explaining, accurately, that helicopters were being shot down from machine gun cross fire.

"I don't want to get my ass shot up either," chimed in another chopper pilot.

It's natural for human fear to take over in any extreme situation. Although sometimes a leader can talk people through their fears by letting them vent their anxieties and then calmly explaining alternatives and walking them through the process of making rational judgments, I didn't have the time. It was one of those situations when you had to lead, follow, or get the hell out of the way. I led. The most expedient solution was to make the pilots more scared of me than the NVA.

I pulled out my sidearm, a Browning 9 mm, walked up to one warrant officer chopper pilot, and said, "I'll blow your brains out right here and now if you don't get me in the air now." He might have thought I was nuts, but he agreed.

By the time we were in the air, the situation was improving due to well-placed artillery and air support. The demoralized, battle-scarred survivors of Company A walked off the Rock Pile before I interceded and were sent to the battalion rear to recover from the loss of their comrades.

While the men were getting some much-needed downtime, I visited a nearby company command post located west of Chu Lai with the battalion commander, a Colonel Coast.

He was a caring, sensitive commander, and I immediately respected him for his concern for the soldiers in his command. Unfortunately, he became the first casualty of war in Vietnam that I personally witnessed. While returning to board our helicopter, which had landed on a steep slope, he did not realize how close to the ground the helicopter blades were rotating. He was hit on the top of his helmet by the rotor blades, which caused a severe brain injury. I was at his bedside for several hours while he fought for his life. It was a horrific experience for me as I shared his suffering to the point where, after learning the wound would be fatal, I begged the attending physician to relieve the colonel of his misery. Although the doctors told me the colonel could not feel a thing, to this day I cannot reconcile that diagnosis with the convulsions the colonel's body was experiencing.

With that terrible vision of the dying Colonel Coast still in my mind, I went to introduce myself to the men of Company A in the rear area where they were recuperating. These young men had just been in a hell of firefight, had lost dozens of their buddies, and had their leadership fail them on that hill. These weren't elite Green Beret noncommissioned officers like those I had commanded in Latin America. These were mostly draftees: young, barely out of basic training, and shell-shocked. They were cursing the U.S. Army, cursing the Vietnam War, and probably cursing Captain Joseph Grano too. After they'd had some time to decompress back in the safer confines of base camp, I called the ninety-eight survivors together.

The morale and cohesiveness of this group of men had to be restored. Company A was going to be back out into the field, with me in command, sooner rather than later. All of our lives would depend on my getting these men to trust me and my decision making so they would follow my orders without hesitation. I had to show them I understood what they were thinking and feeling and would do my best to take care of them. What did these men want? Sure, they wanted to do their duty and be good soldiers. But they also wanted to get home to their families alive and in one piece.

The policy at that time was that when a man had only one month left in his tour, he was pulled out of combat. So I asked the survivors of Company A how many of them had two months or less left in their tour. Eleven men raised their hands. I told them all to get out of formation; I wasn't going to take them back into the field.

I don't know whether there were ever studies to prove it, but the accepted belief among combat leaders in Vietnam was that men generally got killed in either the first two months of their tour or the last two months. That was because in the first two months they didn't know what they were doing, and in the last two they were overly cautious, knowing they would soon be heading home.

I told the remaining eighty-seven men that if they didn't fake illness or injuries and if they came back after "rest and relaxation" on a timely basis, I'd see to it they would get out of the field with three months left in their tours. That promise stabilized the company's morale and gave me time to win the men over.

To turn Company A around, I needed to create an environment of shared sacrifice and mutual respect. The character and personality of a leader sets the tone for an organization, so I began letting Company A know who its new commander was.

I began by engaging my first sergeant. (Sergeants are the true backbones of the army.) I shared with him my priorities and gave him the autonomy to enforce our training and recruitment needs. I also recruited two new platoon leaders, by the names of Orlowski and Montgomery, both Special Forces trained. With these two great officers and my first sergeant, we focused on establishing a sense of pride and esprit de corps among our troops. We reinforced training at every level to include patrolling techniques. We continually insisted on a state of readiness by conducting frequent inspections, many of them unannounced.

The maneuver commander of the American Division would reward the best rifle company with eight cases of beer each month. The "best" was defined by the companies within the division that killed, captured, or wounded the most Vietcong (VC) and NVA, as well as the companies that excelled during inspections. Our company never bought a can of beer.

As I deployed my platoons within different sectors of our area of operations, I insisted that intraday communications be between myself and the platoon leaders. Too many company commanders operated by letting most of the observations within the combat zone be communicated from one radio operator to another. This is a foolish delegation, as you can achieve an assessment or a pulse of the enemy by continually evaluating the signs in the field. Too much gets lost by letting the radio operators screen the dialogue. It is no different in business: you need a pulse, you need to read the signs. My lieutenants reported directly to me, and not unlike any managerial direct report in business, the message was, "Talk to me, lieutenant."

Within twelve days of roaming our area of operations and battling the jungle, I had a sense of where our enemies were operating or hiding. The discovery of an underground enemy hospital by one of my platoons even made headlines in the United States: we captured over eight hundred pounds of medical equipment.

I always selected each of my company's landing zones (LZ) within our area of operations, and I was always the first to enter and the last to leave. By leading by example, establishing a chain of command, and directing my platoon leaders personally, my company of eighty-seven men achieved the impossible: no casualties and the highest kill ratio within the Americal Division, which numbered ten thousand men.

A turning point that helped me win over the group and gave me a bit of a reputation happened during one of my first missions with the company when I let my troops see my sense of humor as well as my willingness to stick my neck out. I got a call from the division commanding officer's helicopter pilot asking for permission to land. The area was still "hot" with some sniping going on, so I responded, "Permission denied."

The pilot called back and repeated, "Requesting permission to land," and then added, "Don't you know who's asking?"

I replied, "I know who's asking, but I don't give a damn. Permission's still denied." In a designated area of operations, or AO, the commander on the ground has the authority to decide, even over a general in the air.

A day later, after the sniping died down, I gave the general's helicopter permission to land when it returned.

The general stormed out of the chopper and headed straight for me.

"Do you know who I am?" he snapped at me.

"Yes, sir," I answered.

"Who the hell do you think you are stopping me from visiting my troops!" he bellowed.

"Sir, we were having contact with snipers," I explained, and pointing to his gleaming belt buckle, said, "You see that big eagle on your stomach? Well, I don't give a damn about you, but those guys are terrible shots. I'm afraid they'll miss you and hit me."

He stared at me for a minute and then burst out laughing.

I worked hard to earn the loyalty and respect of my men—all of my men. I also became quickly known for not tolerating intolerance in the company or even in the battalion. At one point I was named acting S1, which is the staff officer in charge of personnel.

I was asked by the battalion commander to fly back to Duc Pho, to the battalion rear area. Over 125 men in the rear area claimed they were physically impaired and could not perform active duty in combat. Those men, referred to as "on profile," represented more than 25 percent of the battalion, which defied all odds and put the battalion in an unacceptable state of readiness. Upon my arrival I was picked up in a jeep by a buck sergeant named McKenna. I asked him about the unusually high number of soldiers on profile. He responded, "You don't want to know."

As we pulled into the rear area barracks compound, the first thing I observed was a pizza stand. The second was four soldiers exchanging drugs between them. I entered the headquarters of the current S1, a captain. He was very nervous and acted as if he was living in fear. I calmly told him he was to go to the brigade G1 and ask for a reassignment because I was removing him from command. He suggested I had no such authority. I quickly reaffirmed my instructions from the battalion commander.

That evening I called for a formation, or assembly, of the 125 soldiers scattered in the rear area. Only 15 soldiers showed up. I told them to tell the 110 no-shows that each would receive a company Article 15—a nonjudicial punishment by a commander that didn't require a court-martial—and would be charged thirty dollars for not obeying a direct order. The next morning I called another formation, and this time 30 soldiers showed up. I informed them that the remaining 95 soldiers would receive another company Article 15 and would be charged another sixty dollars each. I announced that in the evening there would be yet another formation and any no-show would be charged with a battalion Article 15 offense and would be sent to the brig. That evening all 125 soldiers attended formation.

I instructed them that any genuine disability would be treated, and that those in that category deserved to be assigned to the rear area. All others were to meet with me one-on-one and explain to me why they were not on active duty. The following week constituted the most strenuous test of interpersonal skill I have ever experienced.

My first interview was with an African American soldier who ordained himself "leader of the pack." He informed me that he was the first cousin of H. Rap Brown, an official of the Black Panther Party known for his support of violent actions. He then showed me a .38 caliber pistol in his belt and proceeded to explain what a serious hole in a body a shot from a

.38 could achieve. Against army protocol I responded by leaving my chair, coming around my desk, and knocking out H. Rap Brown's cousin. I immediately called in Sergeant McKenna and asked him what he thought had just happened. He replied that he had never seen a soldier take such an accidental fall.

That evening, out of fear of being "fragged" (killed by a grenade "accidentally" thrown into my tent by my men), I decided to go on the offense. Unannounced, I entered each tent or bunker in the rear area and encountered drug use, misappropriated weapons, and contraband. The saga continued throughout the week until I had approximately ten soldiers arrested and returned over fifty to the front line.

More than half of the soldiers were legitimately on profile, and several had legitimate complaints about discrimination. There were a couple of company commanders whom the men claimed were bigots. After investigating, I discovered these officers were indeed prejudiced and were always assigning African American soldiers to the point position, the most exposed spot on patrol. I had the two company commanders relieved. Having demonstrated that I wouldn't tolerate insubordination from the ranks or prejudice from the officers, I had, I hoped, earned enough respect from the men to get their attention. Now it was time to win their loyalty through effective combat leadership.

To the consternation of my commanders, I would personally lead patrols with soldiers from my command center. That was because I believed that a company commander should be willing to do what he asked a draftee to do: go into harm's way.

One of my earliest observations in Vietnam was that the senior officers would direct a company or platoon to go from point A to point B in the course of a day. This approach not only negated the ability of the unit to patrol the area of operations, but it also put soldiers at undue risk. Advancing in a straight line is much too predictable and makes the flanks highly vulnerable, increasing the likelihood of an ambush. As a company commander, I decided to treat the line between point A and point B as simply an "axis of advance." I instructed my platoons to drop their rucksacks and fan out to the left and right of the "axis" in order to search for the enemy.

My battalion commander was initially perplexed by this strategy. He changed his mind when captured documents from a deceased North Vietnamese officer stated that enemy units in our area of operations were to stay away from Alpha Four-Three. That was my call sign.

It was a great lesson in how to fight a guerrilla war. You don't engage with conventional tactics such as massive battalion sweeps. You deploy in small units as we did in the Green Berets. If you are aggressive and hunt the enemy, the enemy will run from you. If you maneuver en masse and in a straight line, the enemy, in small units, will ambush, kill, and wound your men, and then run and hide until you present yourself again as a target too predictable to ignore.

My company, the same dispirited men who were shattered by their experience on the Rock Pile, had become a crack infantry company. The men who served under me had a sense of confidence that I'd get them home alive. In my time as commander, we suffered a single fatality due to combat. And that came during my final patrol.

One morning, sitting in a helicopter on our way to a new area of operations, I received a radio call from my brand-new battalion commander. A lieutenant colonel from the Pentagon, he had just arrived in Vietnam and had never been in combat before. He excitedly shouted that there were Vietcong near the fire base and wanted to insert my first platoon to engage the enemy. I happened to have with me a New Zealand major who had only three days left to serve in Vietnam. He had insisted on joining us on an operation in order to understand why we were the most successful company in combat. The battalion commander decided to insert my first platoon into the area and have me run the operation from a helicopter known as a command-and-control ship.

As fate would have it, the remainder of my command center, about fifteen soldiers, accustomed to following me into an area of operations, jumped into the helicopters ahead of the first platoon. As a result, I decided that rather than send the helicopters back for the first platoon, I'd enter the area where the battalion commander identified the enemy along with my command center.

Upon landing, I radioed the battalion commander and asked where the enemy was that he had identified. He informed me that five hundred meters from my current position was a Vietcong in a purple shirt, sitting under a tree. I went ballistic. I told the lieutenant colonel that, first, the VC was more than likely already dead and that, second, we would be walking into an ambush. This wasn't long after the My Lai Massacre, in which Lieutenant William Calley had ordered the killing of Vietnamese civilians. (Calley was subsequently tried and convicted of premeditated murder.) With this incident fresh in everyone's minds, the lieutenant colonel stated that he wanted a positive identification and that we were to proceed to the location of the purple-shirted gentleman sitting under the tree.

When a unit moves through jungle terrain, it sends out a soldier who acts as the point man, generally fifty feet in front of the main body. Trailing the point man is a soldier called the slack man. He is generally twenty feet behind the point and thirty feet in front of the main body. His job is to provide cover for the point man by watching his flanks. The officer commanding the unit is generally positioned within the middle of the main body, along with his radio operator, so he can call in artillery or air support if needed.

Typically in an ambush, the enemy is well hidden. They let the point man go by them and begin their ambush by firing on the slack man and the main body in order to maximize the number of people they can engage within the killing zone. Because of my concern for an ambush on this patrol, I instructed my radio operator to stay in position and chose to move up to become the slack man. I also instructed him to knock out the New Zealand major if the "shit hit the fan," as I did not want any heroics from a man with only three days left in Vietnam.

My point man proceeded to move to the designated location. I was twenty feet behind him scanning his left and right flanks when suddenly I heard a popping sound to my left and saw black smoke rise in the air. I yelled out to the main body to "hit the ground," and a tremendous explosion engulfed me. I was thrown fifteen feet in the air and landed sitting in a crater, unable to breathe.

I looked down and saw my left arm hanging from my body by a shred of muscle. I remember thinking to myself, "Well, dummy, you have lost an arm." I put my arm inside my shirt so it wouldn't fall off. I could feel my left boot filling up with blood and actually had a feeling of hope, believing that since I could feel the flow of blood, I might not lose my left leg. I had been wearing a gold cross around my neck and, incredibly, I now found it sitting in my right hand.

We had been hit by a booby trap built from a grenade and a 105 mm artillery round. The enemy had placed it in a position where we would have to travel to check out the VC in the purple shirt sitting under a tree. I was in the center of the crater caused by the explosion. My point man was screaming in pain, and the man I'd replaced as slack man was behind me nearly unconscious. I never saw the New Zealand major again but can only assume he was knocked out by my radio operator.

Our medic had just arrived in Vietnam the day before and appeared to be going into shock from witnessing his first casualties. Once again faced with fearful inaction in a crisis requiring immediate action, I used the same technique that had worked so well in getting me to the Rock Pile many months before. I took out my sidearm with my right hand and told the medic I would personally shoot him if he didn't go to the screaming point man and administer morphine to ease his pain.

I did not realize the extent of my injuries. Besides my almost severed left arm and severely wounded left leg, my right knee was shattered, I had nineteen broken bones, a large chunk of metal was embedded in my forehead, penetrating the sinus cavity, and there were multiple shrapnel wounds throughout my body. The helicopter that inserted us returned to pick up my point man, slack man, and yours truly. Fortunately for me, my anger prevented me from going into shock. I was able to keep the young soldier I'd replaced as slack man alive with heart massage and mouth-to-mouth resuscitation during the thirty-minute ride to the hospital.

We were flown to the army hospital in Chu Lai on the east coast of Vietnam. When I arrived, I was greeted by a doctor wearing Bermuda shorts and a sweatshirt, both speckled with sand from the beach. He told me I would lose my left arm and, more than likely, my left leg.

Annoyed at his flippancy and angered by his appearance, I told him that when I got to the main hospital in Okinawa, they could do what they had to do but that he wasn't going to amputate anything. Fortunately, twenty-five soldiers from my company had run to the hospital from our base camp when they heard about the ambush. In front of the beach bum doctor, I told my twenty-five soldiers to shoot him if he amputated any of my limbs while I was under anesthesia. They locked and loaded their M16s.

Nine hours after being wounded, I came out of the operating room wrapped up like a mummy but with all my limbs. The young man I'd kept alive on the helicopter died from a piece of shrapnel the size of a dime, and my point man ultimately lost an eye and a leg.

The division commander was standing by my bed. He said, "Joe, we are losing our best company commander. Now would you please tell your soldiers to stand down." I laughed, said, "Yes, sir," and told the general I could run the company by radio. That evening the new battalion commander came to the hospital with tears in his eyes. When interviewed by the general, I never reported the lieutenant colonel's mindless order that put my command center in harm's way. He remained grateful even after I'd left the service.

I remained in the hospital in Chu Lai for three days. The doctors there did not attempt to realign my broken bones or close my many open wounds. Each day they added more gauze to my mummified body, explaining that most wounds received in Vietnam were highly susceptible to infection and could not be fully treated until the doctors were sure they were free from infection. They also informed me that my left leg would be saved but I would more than likely lose my left arm.

I had decided to stop taking pain medication the third day after being wounded because it was dragging me into the bowels of depression. I knew that if I had any chance of not being a cripple, I had to force my torn muscles back into alignment, and to do that, I needed a clear mind. I would have to remain positive and learn to deal with the pain.

On the fourth day, I was sent on a small jet to Okinawa, where the army had a major medical facility. The plane was furnished with cots aligned like a group of bunk beds. I remember being very embarrassed because I could not move to relieve myself. The nurses on the plane were unbelievably understanding and caring.

When I arrived in Okinawa, I was placed on a gurney and wheeled into the hospital. I recall being very confused as they wheeled me to several floors below the main floor. The farther we descended down the underground floors, the thicker the walls got. After going some three floors underground, I faced the purest physical challenge of my life.

Lying in the hallway on my gurney, I was staring into a room where a young soldier, who had lost a foot, was lying on a hospital bed. He held a small canister in his hand and was breathing in the gas that subsequently caused a giddy, euphoric reaction. He was laughing and chatting with a major, apparently an orthopedic surgeon, and a large sergeant, apparently a medic. As the strapping sergeant held the young soldier down, the major began tearing off the bandages that surrounded the area where his foot had once been. The young soldier began to scream in agony, begging God to end his misery. I had never witnessed such human suffering before, not even in combat. After his ordeal, which lasted approximately ten minutes, he returned to his gas canister and his euphoric state.

After the young soldier was wheeled out of the room, I was wheeled in and lifted onto the bed. The major explained to me that all those layers of bandages that encompassed my body like a mummy's were purposely allowed to accumulate. Coupled with the dried blood, they formed the equivalent of a scab over my wounds. By stripping these artificial scabs, they would be tearing away any infection, along with all the accompanying nerve endings—hence, the pain. He stated that wounded patients generally had to endure this process three times before all infection had worked out of the area and surgery could be performed.

The sergeant came to my side and handed me the gas canister. I told him to "stick it where the sun doesn't shine" as I contemplated what was about to happen, remembering the young soldier without a foot and me with both legs, my left arm, and my chest about to be peeled. I told the sergeant and the major to give me a towel to bite on and suggested that with a little luck, I might pass out from the pain. I wasn't so lucky.

Of my half-hour in hell, I still have two vivid memories. One is when I came close to connecting a well-aimed punch from my one good arm with the sergeant's chin. The other is when, at the end of the process, the sergeant held the fingers of my left hand while the major pushed down on my left bicep to pull the extruding bones from my forearm back into my skin. That hurt. Unbelievably it turned out that I had no infection and never had to go through the ordeal again.

That night the orthopedic surgeon came to my bedside with a full bottle of Haig and Haig scotch. He said he'd never met such a crazy "son of a bitch" as me and that he wanted to share a drink with me. That was one pain remedy I just couldn't turn down.

I had sacrificed for my country and left a lot of blood on the ground in Vietnam, but I also gained a great deal from my military service. One lesson was a perspective on war.

Although I never regretted going into combat and if the uniform still fit, I would serve today if asked, I will also state, if asked, that I did not agree with the way we fought the war. If you want to engage in a police or political action, send in trained volunteer soldiers such as Green Berets or Navy SEALs. The moment you send in a draftee or a reservist, then you must declare war and fight to win.

I also learned that war should be avoided whenever possible. The taking of human life should never be trivialized, and men and women should not be reduced to the Neanderthal state required to fight a war unless there is no other option. Ever since Vietnam, I have been incapable of killing an animal for sport. If and when war is deemed to be necessary to defend or liberate, we as a nation must be prepared to win the war with defined certainty. That is the best way to discourage the next conflict and the only true justification for a soldier's sacrifice.

War also gave me the priceless gift of perspective. Ever since, I've been able to remain sober and dispassionate in the face of the most trying, traumatic, and potentially disastrous personal and business situations because I can honestly say, "It's not Vietnam," and mean it.

I learned as well that potential can be found in surprising places and nurtured until it blossoms. I entered the military as a tough kid who had some innate but rudimentary leadership skills. The army polished my natural gifts, gave me an arsenal of tools and techniques to use in winning the hearts and minds of subordinates, and taught me to approach crises as problems requiring solutions. Combat in the rain forests of Latin America and the jungles of Vietnam was my graduate school. It forged who I am today. I learned how to take a dispirited and disunited group of individuals, turn them into a motivated and driven team, and lead them to victory against all the odds.

There have been times over the years when I have applied this lesson in the corporate world. I have pulled individuals into the financial services industry from outside or have taken young people and "jumped them up in rank." Those who are not immersed in the legacy thinking of an organization can provide the fresh thinking and exuberance necessary to bring originality and creativity to a firm and keep it from becoming moribund. Of course, sometimes they made mistakes, but by providing them with "air cover" and making sure they didn't overextend themselves, I usually got the kind of fresh perspective needed to succeed. What they didn't know, they were eager to learn.

When I had left Hartford, I thought I'd do my duty as an infantryman for two years and return to Connecticut to finish college as a more mature individual ready to study, not just party. When I finally headed back from the military, it was six, not two, years later. I was a Green Beret captain and a combat veteran. I brought home not just added maturity, but a body full of shrapnel and enough broken bones and torn muscles, tendons, and ligaments to qualify me as 60 percent disabled. Instead of a sheepskin, I had a Bronze Star with a V for valor. Without a college education and with severe physical limitations, I did not know what my future would hold.

"When people are frenetic and scared or emotional, [Grano] is the opposite. He instills a sense of calmness, a sense that everything is going to be just fine."

—ROBERT SILVER, FORMER PRESIDENT OF UBS WEALTH MANAGEMENT SERVICES

Chapter Three

Be the Eternal Optimist

When dealing with crises or when revitalizing a poorly performing organization, you must position yourself as an eternal optimist. In the darkest moments, your subordinates are looking to you, as their leader, for a solution—for a bright light to follow out of the doom-and-gloom tunnel. They expect you to be aware of the facts, regardless of how ugly they may be. But they also look to you for the leadership to solve the problem.

Successful leaders are those who position themselves as an extension of the solution rather than just the articulation of the problem. There are many times when the severity of a situation will threaten to drag you into the depths of pessimism. The optimist says, No. Understanding that pessimism will only exacerbate the problem. I believe good leaders live by the motto "Can Do" while mediocre managers live by "Can't Be Done."

Being positive, optimistic, and focusing on "can" rather than "can't" leads to a winning perspective that permeates an organization as well as your own persona. A winning attitude spreads quickly throughout your firm, and it echoes externally as well as internally. I have always informed my employees that you cannot espouse greatness externally unless you believe it internally.

I have never doubted the potential of optimism after experiencing how the power of the mind and positive attitude got me through the most difficult period in my life.

I was wounded in August and arrived back in the United States on September 2, 1972. The doctors at Fort Devens, Massachusetts, excitedly told me that I would not lose my leg, though they warned me that my left arm might have to go. I asked when I could go home. My wife was still at my parents' house and about to give birth to our first daughter. The leading physician laughed and said that with a lot of luck, maybe in five months. He said that I had to learn to walk again, and I couldn't begin *that* until my bones and muscles had healed and realigned. Once they saw how out of alignment my body had become after healing, they could teach me how to deal with my new condition. Until I could walk on my own, I'd have to stay in the hospital.

That was an unacceptable answer. First, I refused to accept just lying back and allowing my body to heal in a manner that could leave me a cripple. And second, I wouldn't allow myself to be stuck in the hospital for five months. To get out of the hospital, I had to walk, so I resolved to do just that.

Some members of the New York National Guard were serving their compulsory two weeks of training at the hospital, and each evening I convinced four of them to lift me up so I could learn how to balance on a cane and take a couple of steps. It was excruciating, but I disciplined myself to just deal with the pain. The efforts tore many of my stitches, but I believe they helped keep my muscles from misaligning permanently.

Seven days later, on the morning of September 9, as the doctors approached my room, I had the National Guardsmen lift me out of bed. I walked four feet and, standing right in front of the doctors, asked them to send me home. Realizing I wasn't going to be a cooperative patient, they literally threw me out of the hospital, declaring they would not be responsible if I injured myself further by pushing myself too hard before my body had sufficient time to heal. The town of Wethersfield, Connecticut, sent an ambulance, along with my father, to pick me up, and all 128 pounds of what had been a 185-pound Green Beret were brought home.

I was deposited on a couch downstairs in my parents' home and slept for seventy-two hours straight. When I awoke, I told my family that if I fell, I would appreciate their helping me back to my feet. But if they interfered with my recovery regimen in any other way, I would move to a hotel room. I practiced my walking as much as the pain allowed. Four days later, I climbed the stairs to the second-floor bedroom. It took me eight hours, and afterward I slept for forty-eight hours. It took me ten hours to return down the stairs. I had to maneuver backward in order to anchor my one good arm on the stair railing. After that effort, I slept for twenty-four hours.

Thirty days after my arrival home, I returned to the hospital at Fort Devens and slowly hobbled up to the head physician. The doctor dropped his clipboard on the floor and, with a frozen expression on his face, told me to return home since they could not do as much for me as I was doing for myself.

Six months later, I was discharged from the army with a 60 percent permanent disability. A soldier who loses a leg receives 40 percent. The doctors' prognosis was that I would never lift anything heavier than a milk bottle with my left arm, that I would need braces on both legs, and that I would develop a crippling form of arthritis.

Today I use both arms to work out with two hundred pounds of weights. I wear no leg braces. Unfortunately, the arthritis is flourishing. I can be sitting in a cool room yet start sweating as my body's system works to burn off pain that remains with me to this day. I took more than just pain away from my recovery process: I maintain a belief in the power of the mind and a positive outlook. I believe the only reason that I'm now able to use all my limbs is that I refused to accept the alternative.

I had never lacked confidence. But it had always been confidence in my physical prowess, my intellect, and my ability to lead and inspire. To this package was now added confidence in my will to win and overcome adversity. I might have been physically devastated, but I was psychologically more powerful than ever before.

Convalescing from my wounds, I was bored and faced with the reality of needing to find a career. I was twenty-two years old, medically incapacitated, my only real training was in engaging the enemy, and I had no college degree. The owner of Rainbow Realty in nearby Newington, Connecticut, took pity on me and gave me a shot as a real estate salesman. Despite becoming a top salesman, I concluded after six months that real estate was not for me: it just was not sufficiently challenging.

I also realized that due to my physical condition, I no longer had a future in the military. My old division commander discouraged me from leaving the army. He confirmed my promotion to major and intimated there could be a general's star in my future if I came along with him to his new assignment in the Pentagon. "What's the assignment?" I asked.

"Logistics," he said. "And you'll need to forget about Special Forces."

I said thanks but no thanks. At the time, I thought my physical problems would preclude me from ever serving in a combat element of the army.

One morning while working at the real estate office, I read an ad in the local newspaper for a stockbroker trainee position at Merrill Lynch, which started with a six-month training course. I immediately sensed that this could be the further education I desperately needed and could lead me to a new career path. That very day I gimped into Merrill Lynch's Hartford office and applied for the position.

In those days, in order to be hired as a stockbroker trainee, you needed to take an aptitude test and were required to go to New York City to be interviewed by a psychologist at Merrill Lynch's headquarters. I did well on the test and believed I did well on the headquarters interview. But to my surprise and disappointment, I was told that even though I'd done well, I needed either to go back to school for a degree or get some business experience before I could be accepted.

Fortunately for me, in the 1970s the branch office managers at Merrill Lynch wielded more power than the home office. The Hartford manager, Herb Hedick, said that due to my war record, I had a job with him. However his office was full, and I might have to wait up to six months for an opening. He asked if I would consider working at the New Haven office, which had immediate openings, and offered to recommend me to that office's manager. I did not know a soul in New Haven, so I had no network on which to draw in building up my business. I accepted nevertheless.

After my three months of in-office training, I went to New York for three months of intensive classroom training, where I was taught economics, corporate finance, taxation, products, and prospecting. Today broker trainees are trained for only three months, with an emphasis on products and prospecting. It doesn't make sense to me that the industry has responded to a proliferation of new, complex products, and a much more complex market environment, by cutting the training period in half.

I became a stockbroker in 1972. To put it mildly, the stock market wasn't doing very well. That year marked the beginning of a secular bear market that lasted approximately ten years. This was not a bubble bursting, like the 1987 crash, when the market experienced a precipitous decline and subsequently recovered. Being in the market in 1972 was like going through slow, consistent water torture. For my first two years in the business, the market declined 48 percent. Over the ensuing ten years, the market remained in the throes of a bear market.

My naiveté about the market condition was a blessing since it helped me approach my position as a new stockbroker with my positive attitude intact. Since I hadn't experienced the previous bull market, I had no memory of what had been, or what could have been. All I knew was how the market was right then.

Besides the power of optimism, launching my stockbroker career at a time when the market was in a long-term down cycle taught me another good lesson: crisis really does equal opportunity—at least for those with an optimistic approach. In tough times, when everyone around you tends to hide from their clients, a fabulous opportunity arises for those who are willing to engage clients when they need you most.

Think about it. Why would a client leave his or her current broker in good times when that broker is doing well for the client? The answer is that they most likely wouldn't. It's when clients are unhappy with their results or when they're not being serviced appropriately that they're open to a new relationship. Many of my fellow brokers shied away from client contact because they didn't know what to advise in a market they'd never experienced before. Other brokers left the business because of the pressure. A window of opportunity opened for me because I had no such insecurities and was able to thrive under pressure. I became a refreshing alternative for clients who felt abandoned by their brokers.

There's an obvious lesson here for those in a service business in today's recessionary economy. Long and deep recessions are a time when many businesses fail and many fortunes are lost. But they're also a time when new businesses can gain market share and become successful and new fortunes can be made.

During my New York training, I developed a plan for building my business once I received my license. I evaluated what knowledge I would need to provide added value to wealthy investors. How could I differentiate myself? Most wealthy investors already had a stockbroker or two and, other than their being dissatisfied with their current advisor, what would motivate them to switch to me?

I began with a prospecting plan. I wasn't then, and am not now, an advocate of cold calling. The thousands of financial advisors who enter the business every year all gravitate to the same doctors, lawyers, and corporate presidents. These people are inundated with cold calls because they are readily identifiable and accessible. My strategy was to service the affluent who were underserviced or, at a minimum, harder to find.

At that time there were over 1 million millionaires in the United States, and most weren't doctors, lawyers, or corporate presidents. Studies of wealthy people revealed that 75 percent of all financial assets were in the hands of people fifty years of age and older. I needed to find where, if anywhere, they were concentrated. Was it the country club? Affluent senior housing?

I honed in on two targets. The first was the sole proprietor: the dry cleaner, the gas station owner, the owner of a private manufacturing business, and any other successful entrepreneur. I thought my upbringing, military career, and personality would help me make a connection with these potential clients. I thought, at the time, that I'd more easily relate to them than the doctors, lawyers, and corporate executives.

The second target was a common residential location. The owner of the gas station with grease under his fingernails may not want to be a member of a country club, but he invariably lives in a nice home. So my prospecting strategy assumed that birds of a feather flocked together. I prospected streets with expensive homes. Sure, the doctor and lawyer probably lived on the same street, but I was really after their next-door neighbor: the entrepreneur who owned a number of hardware stores or a successful contracting business.

I gathered census data by occupation and street address. When I found several affluent occupations living on a particular street, I concluded the birds were flocking and created a mailing list of every household on the street.

I supplemented this direct mail strategy with a series of forums and seminars. I invited affluent individuals to a seminar discussing, for instance, changes in the tax law, or perhaps how to bequeath a larger percentage of their assets to their loved ones net of estate taxes. I gave these forums on Saturdays—one session in the morning and one in the afternoon—to accommodate both the shoppers and the golfers. I presented at a location convenient to my prospects, say a clubhouse or a rented conference room in their community. I knew I needed to go to them rather than expecting them to come to my office. My goal was to send out three hundred pieces of direct mail a week, have a seminar or forum once a quarter, and open one new account a day—all extremely optimistic targets.

When my office manager objected to paying the postage costs for a trainee to send out three hundred mailers a week, my response was to make a deal: in any given month that I led the office in new account openings, the manager paid my postage bill. If I wasn't number one in a given month, I paid the postage bill. My manager jumped at the deal because it offered him a win-win situation. I was confident I'd rarely have to pay for the postage.

My direct mail campaign to affluent households residing on affluent streets yielded bona fide leads on a daily basis. My number one mailer was an invitation to receive a booklet entitled, "Investing for Tax Free Income." That mailer earned the extraordinary return of over 25 percent, clearly the right message sent to the right people.

I also learned that I dramatically increased my returns if I hand-addressed the envelopes. Think of your own reaction. You never automatically throw out a hand-addressed envelope sent to you, do you? You always open it.

When a return coupon showed up on my desk, I sent the booklet, my card, and a personalized note to the prospect. After all these years I remember the note by heart:

> *Dear Mr. Jones,*
>
> *I am confident the enclosed materials will be useful in analyzing Municipal Bonds as a tax minimization vehicle. I will call you in the near future to determine if I can be of any further assistance. In the meantime, please contact me for any additional information you may require.*
>
> *Cordially,*
>
> *Joe Grano*

I placed the stack of returned coupons in my day calendar ten days forward. During that ten-day waiting period, my sales assistant found me these prospects' occupation and telephone numbers. When I walked into the office ten days later, those coupons with a work telephone number became the basis for my "day calls." Those with only a home telephone number became my "night calls." I disciplined myself to open at least one account a day. I worked normal business hours, plus three evenings a week, plus a half-day on Saturday. Of course, there were a few days when I hadn't opened an account by 9:00 P.M., and I called some distant cousin in order to open my daily account and go home. But that was always my last resort because I didn't want relatives as clients; they exacerbated the pressure of the job.

For me the most fruitful time for prospecting was between 7:00 P.M. and 9:00 P.M. Because I had sent a personalized note to the prospect ten days earlier, my call was generally answered with, "Yes, Joe, I received your note but I haven't had time to read the book yet." I responded that the most important page in the book dealt with tax brackets and the equivalent after-tax return comparisons between taxable and nontaxable interest. From that point in the conversation, I'd seek an appointment with the prospect.

I was right about rarely having to pay the postage bills. My optimism, a good strategy, and lots of hard work helped me achieve my goal. At the end of my first year as a broker, I led my office in new account openings. Despite my early success, I was called into the sales manager's office. He proceeded to tell me that I should focus on prospecting unions. I asked him why. And he answered, "Because they come from under the same rock you do." I did not lose my temper, but he chose to quit the firm when I became his boss three years later.

Along with my prospecting plan, I developed a line of products and services that would best serve the affluent, entrepreneurial clients I was pursuing. By being knowledgeable in relevant products and services, I could differentiate myself from the sea of stockbrokers. I wanted to be known as a specialist in the areas most important to wealthy people. I confidently came up with my own definition on what it meant to be a specialist: no one else in my office knew more about the product or service than I did. There were more than two hundred products in the brokerage business, and no one can be a specialist in that many. I decided to acquire expertise in five product groups and approximately five products in each group that were germane to wealthy individuals. I concluded that specialization in twenty-five products was achievable, and that if I selected them judiciously, I'd have no competition within the community.

My five product groups were tax-related products, retirement plans, insurance, asset management, and stocks and bonds. I thought of my selections as the fingers on one's hand. If I was discussing with a prospect the tax minimization benefits of a municipal bond, a bond swap, an installment sale, a charitable remainder trust, or an estate plan, then more likely than not, the prospect was somewhere in the private sector as a sole proprietor or a corporate professional. That being the case, the prospect might then need a product from my second finger or group: a retirement plan, for example. Then, moving to my third finger, most affluent investors are underinsured, or need tax deferrals available within insurance annuity programs, or perhaps an affordable second-to-die policy to mitigate prospective estate taxes. My fourth finger or group dealt with asset management. A financial advisor cannot effectively follow a stock in China or Brazil. But as globalization continues as a reality, a larger and larger percentage of asset allocation models will commit to a global tranche. (A tranche is one of a number of securities that are offered as a package.) A mutual fund, an asset manager, a hedge fund, funds of funds, and even private equity have a place in an affluent investor's portfolio. My role was to prescreen and delegate to these entities a portion of my clients' assets to manage and subsequently monitor their performance. My fifth group was stocks and bonds. By virtue of my title, I had to specialize in these two products. Besides, if a wealthy person was investing in a tax-related product, needed a retirement plan, was looking at supplementing his or her insurance policies, or was going to engage an asset manager, he or she invariably owned stocks and bonds. Therefore, every affluent client could possibly need all five product groups and potentially buy five products.

There are tens of thousands of stocks and bonds to select from. For stocks I developed a selection process that had four criteria. First, my firm's research had to have a "strong buy" or "buy" recommendation on the stock. Second, I followed a minimum of eight stocks: two would match a client's objective for growth, two would match an objective of income, two would be for a combination of income and growth, and two for speculation. My third criterion was that these be companies that would benefit from a long-term secular trend. (A secular market trend is a long-term trend of anywhere from five to twenty-five years.) Health care stocks, for example, benefit from longer life spans. Fourth, I had to love the stocks for their inherent value.

I didn't hesitate to build large positions in these companies, matching the stock to my client's investment objective. When I no longer liked a company, I would sell the stock and replace it with another. Whenever I was asked, "What do you like?" I would respond with a question of my own: "What's your objective: growth, income, growth and income, or speculation?" I would have two choices for each objective in case the client already owned one of the two.

For bonds, I preferred local issues, having a tax-free and taxable bond for long-term, intermediate-term, and short-term duration. Every week I would price the bonds so I could quote a price and yield for the client.

Clients, whenever surveyed, are consistent in complaining that financial advisors are quick to advise what and when to buy but never call about what and when to sell. The biggest secret of humankind is when to sell. Too often a purchased security is allowed to fall into the depths of hell before the client is told to get out of that position. Too often an appreciated stock is sold prematurely because it's easier to say to a client, "We made money; let's get out of Dodge." I always followed the adage that if a stock is not good enough to buy, then it is not good enough to hold. If a stock I recommended went up and I was still willing to buy more, I left it alone and let the gains run. If it was no longer a buy because the price was too high, I sold it and took my gains. If a stock went down and I still liked it, I bought more. If I didn't like the way the stock was acting and I wasn't willing to buy more, I sold it, took my losses, and looked for the next opportunity. If I sold a stock, I immediately replaced it with a new one to bring my "inventory" back up to eight.

Besides relying on this methodology, I was privileged to have a mentor in my office. Elliot Gluntz was the quintessential broker: a gentleman who loved the business, loved his clients, and conducted himself with the highest degree of ethics and integrity. He taught me that you never do anything for a commission. If you do the right thing for your clients, commissions take care of themselves. I was able to teach him one thing, however.

One day toward the end of my second year in production, I asked him how he could possibly service the seven books of client accounts he had on a shelf above his desk. They had to total some thousand clients or more. He responded by saying to me, "Joe, I worked hard at opening those accounts, and it doesn't take much to answer the phone when one of them calls."

A year later, when I passed Elliot in productivity, I told him he was wrong about holding on to that many clients because answering those calls all day precluded him from calling out. I believed I needed to continually prospect for good, new clients and to proactively service my best clients, neither of which I could do if I was relegated to being an administrator.

Think of an hourglass: hundreds of clients stored at the top of the glass and hundreds of products stored at the bottom of the glass. The stockbroker is smack in the middle: a very narrow funnel connecting the clients and products. Only so much can flow through the narrow funnel.

Rather than do a disservice to small and/or inactive accounts, I culled my book each year. I passed the accounts I gave up to a young eager broker who I knew would service them diligently. When some of those accounts grew and turned out to be big, I didn't have any regret. I was just happy things worked for both the client and the younger broker. I needed to stay focused on my key clients and their related accounts, regardless of size, and also continue to seek out new key client relationships. I believed that the sooner I moved from a shotgun approach to a rifle approach, the sooner my production would grow exponentially. And that's what happened.

By my third full year as a financial advisor I was the biggest producer in my office, in the city of New Haven, and in the state of Connecticut. I was in the top twenty producers in the entire country. I ultimately led the firm in opening new accounts by averaging thirty-six per month. My optimism had once again been rewarded.

This brief period was one of the most important in my life, as it shaped me physically, mentally, and put me on the path to the career that would define the next forty years of my life. I managed to recover far more quickly and more fully from my combat wounds than anyone expected and become a successful stockbroker during a secular bear market. Both achievements defied the odds. I learned firsthand how crucial it is to exercise the awesome power of the mind and to never underestimate the power of a positive attitude. At any number of points, my life could have taken a very different turn.

If I had allowed myself to go into shock when I was so severely wounded in the jungles of Vietnam, they would have taken my limbs at the field hospital and I would be a double amputee today.

If I hadn't rejected the depressing pain pills they offered me in the hospital, I am certain I would be crippled today, because I wouldn't have had the mental or physical strength to force my muscles and bones back into alignment.

If I hadn't taken a positive proactive approach toward rehabilitation once I returned to the United States, someone would have to carry my suitcase for me today.

If I hadn't persevered to become a broker in spite of a rejection for not having a college degree, I wouldn't have become a stockbroker.

Once I became a broker, if I had let terrible market conditions or the narrow-minded advice of my sales manager deter me, I never would have become a top-performing financial advisor and entered management.

And if I hadn't been able to accomplish all this on my own thanks to my optimism, I never would have been able to create positive, empowered cultures at Merrill Lynch and then PaineWebber.

I left a great deal on that battlefield in Vietnam. But I gained more psychologically than I lost physically. In overcoming my disability and launching a successful career, I had faced two challenges that could not solely be overcome by strength and stamina. These were not public tests of my ability to lead and inspire others, but very private tests of my own spirit and will. I came away from them not just with reinforced self-confidence but with new insights into human nature.

"Joe brings with him a lot of passion, a lot of energy, a lot of ideas. He stretches any organization he's a part of. He has the ability to connect with people like no one else I've ever met. This guy doesn't just talk it, he lives it. That's Joe—the first guy on, the last guy off."

—MARK SUTTON, FORMER CHAIRMAN
AND CEO OF UBS AMERICAS

Chapter Four

RECONCILE YOURSELF TO SELFISHNESS

There exists a very simple tenet that, surprisingly, many organizations and managers fail to embrace. It's that people tend to do what is in their interest. To be an effective leader, you must reconcile yourself to selfishness, even use it as a tool. If you're asking individuals to materially act in a certain way or perform a particular function, then their compensation should, at least in part, reflect their performance in fulfilling the desired task. If compensation practices are not in direct support of strategy, management will be at cross purposes with its subordinates. The manner in which you compensate and motivate your subordinates must support and drive the activities you wish them to perform. People ultimately do what they are paid to do.

I knew this instinctively back when I was trying to rebuild the morale of Company A. Their self-interest was getting out of combat as soon as possible while still doing their duty. My promise to shorten their time in the field was the right compensation to motivate them to fulfill my goal: making the company combat effective. Throughout my career, I've applied this lesson every time I needed to effect change or shift strategy. I've made sure I compensate people in a manner that directly supports where I want them to bring the organization.

My rapid success in the field didn't go unnoticed by people at the headquarters of Merrill Lynch. At the end of my third year in production, I was invited to attend a think-tank session at headquarters in New York with seventeen other large producers from around the country. Because of our success, we were asked to help the firm create some new products and services for key clients that would foster the growth of Merrill Lynch and its brokers. The group honed in on a concierge type of centralized service that would include investment advice for high-net-worth clients. This would be done not by the broker but by a central corporate team.

I was the only dissenter among the group. That was because I saw immediately that the plan ran counter to the self-interests of brokers. I explained that the value of a broker was the advice and counsel he or she provided to a client. If we were to fully delegate that advice and counsel to a central department of whiz kids, we would be commoditizing ourselves and diluting the importance of the broker-client relationships on which our brokers depended. I stressed that we couldn't provide a relationship-based, value-added experience for a client by sending that client to a group of bright strangers trained to methodically deal with thousands of clients. I explained that I often pitched very wealthy people by saying to them: "You don't need me to make you money; you are already very good at it. You need me to be very good at preserving it for you and your loved ones." I said the people at headquarters would be surprised at how many very rich people responded by saying, "Finally, someone who understands what I want and need."

At the end of the day, Merrill Lynch rolled out the new service. As I predicted, the brokers totally rejected it, and it failed. The cost of that failure today would be tens of millions of dollars.

Subsequent to the failure, I received a call from senior management. They commented that I seemed to have an unusual pulse on what brokers and key clients needed and asked if I'd consider becoming the director of marketing services in the home office. I would be managing market planning, market evaluation, advertising, and sales promotion: from targeting our markets, to new product development, to segmentation strategies and pricing. This would be a new, challenging world for me. They offered me a salary of twenty-five thousand dollars a year, which I summarily rejected. Yes, it was an opportunity, but I was making a multiple of that as a producer. And while I had a management ego, my many surgeries after my wounds had not included a frontal lobotomy. I had my own self-interest too. After rejecting them three times, I agreed to leave production to become a manager for fifty thousand dollars a year. It was March 1976 and I had begun my escalation up the corporate ladder, thanks in some measure to having understood what clients wanted and what was in the best interests of the brokers who served them.

Another opportunity came when I was charged with changing the entire basis of our brokers' compensation. Our strategy decision at Merrill Lynch was to move our stockbrokers from a predominantly transactional interface with clients to one based on relationships. Traditionally brokers were compensated solely by a formula percentage of the commissions generated, and until 1974, all firms and all stockbrokers charged the same minimum commissions for a trade. In 1974, negotiated rates were approved, and standard rates were now subject to discounting. We concluded that revenues would steadily decline if we didn't move away from a pure transactional interface.

We responded to this looming crisis by redirecting our value proposition from being trade-centric to one that was advice-centric. We stressed that we offered what discount and electronic brokers could not: the advice and counsel of a fellow human being. This was the foundation of the relationship I had so many months earlier unsuccessfully warned headquarters not to ignore. Now they had come around to my own beliefs.

We already knew that there was a correlation between the assets that a client entrusted to us and the amount of commissions those assets generated, formally known as the return on assets (ROA). With the exception of a small percentage of active trading accounts, the ROAs were quite predictable. In a good market back then, ROAs were 2 percent of assets. So for $1 million of client assets held at the firm, a broker could expect twenty thousand dollars in commissions. In a bad market, the ROA would drop to 1 percent, or ten thousand dollars, in commissions for a $1 million account. Today, due to competitive rates, ROAs are 1 percent in a good market and fifty basis points in a bad market. (A basis point, the unit of measure used in the financial services industry, equals .01 percent or .0001.) The pragmatist in me concluded that in order to offset price deterioration and mitigate the prospect of poor market conditions, we needed to encourage our stockbrokers or financial advisors to gather more of their client's assets. If a financial advisor has $100 million of client assets under his or her control in a good market, he or she will generate $1 million in commissions with an ROA of 1 percent. In a bad market, if the financial advisor increased the asset base to $200 million, the advisor would still produce $1 million in commission despite a drop in the ROA to fifty basis points. Gathering more client assets could also add the ancillary benefit of increased client loyalty. The more of a client's financial assets that you control, the less likely the client will leave, and of course, the more loyal the client is to the firm, the less likely the financial advisor will leave to go to a competitive firm.

In theory, the gathering of additional client assets was an intelligent response to a more competitive marketplace for both the firm and the financial advisors. The challenge was how to get the financial advisors to change their approach to clients and ask for an order that would not accrue the immediate commission to which the advisor was accustomed. The answer was to use the brokers' self-interest.

At Merrill Lynch, we decided to shift a portion of the advisors' pay from 100 percent commission based to partially based on net new assets collected. At the end of each year, we totaled the aggregate value of all the client assets held at the firm by each financial advisor. At the end of the following year, we totaled the aggregate value of assets again, adjusted up or down based on market appreciation or depreciation for each security. This year-to-year comparison would give us a net gain or loss of total assets under control. We would then pay the advisor a percentage on the net gain in assets. For example, we would give an advisor who had a net gain of $10 million in assets a bonus of ½ of 1 percent of the $10 million, or $50,000. That was then, and is still today, a significant amount of money, and it served to catch advisors' attention and focus.

We also decided to pay the advisor $25,000 of that $50,000 in cash and hold back the remaining $25,000 in a deferred compensation account that vested over five years. If the advisor achieved the same result each year for five years, $125,000 would accrue in the account. If the advisor left to go to the competition, he or she would lose $100,000 of the $125,000.

The realignment of compensation to directly support our asset-gathering strategy produced dramatic results for the firm. We avoided the feared crisis and potential deterioration in advisor morale by working with, rather than against, their self-interest. We also became number one measured against all competitive bulge bracket brokerage firms in productivity, number one in assets per financial advisor, and number one in market share growth, and we had the lowest turnover rate of financial advisors. (*Bulge bracket firm* was a term used to describe a member of the group of the largest and most profitable investment banks in the world.)

It's vital to the long-term viability of an organization to balance this acceptance and use of selfishness. A company that becomes nothing more than a combination of competing self-interests will eventually tear itself apart. So while a leader needs to become reconciled to selfishness and use it as a tool in meeting goals, he or she also needs to find a way to keep these self-interested groups from battling over a limited pool of resources. The answer is a counterbalancing pursuit of fairness.

This fairness extends beyond just rejecting bigotry and religious intolerance. (That, in fact, should be a sine qua non.) I learned how to apply fairness in business as a balance to self-interest from Dan Tully, my boss at Merrill Lynch. Dan preached an exceptional philosophy. He believed that you must run a business as a partnership with three dominant partners: your clients, your shareholders, and your employees. All three are stakeholders in your enterprise, and all share a common denominator: they are people first. That means they are all at least partially motivated by self-interest.

Dan taught me that every major decision a leader makes has to be fair and equitable to all three. If you cut a deal that overly favors one, you are automatically stiffing the other two. Leadership, then, is partly a constant balancing act, addressing the self-interests of each partner while not being unfair to the other two partners. I adhered to this approach in everything from my compensation policies for employees, to pricing models for clients, to earnings goals that potentially would reward our investors or shareholders with a commensurate return on their investment.

This philosophy postures you and your organization to take a pragmatic and fair approach toward all of your constituents. It signals that your organization believes it is not about what you can get away with but, rather, what is fair and equitable. Many new courses have evolved within our best universities that address corporate ethics. Frankly, I believe that if the culture of any firm recognizes human self-interest and also embraces this equal, fair treatment for each of the major partners, corporations will automatically behave ethically.

Later, when I took the reins of PaineWebber, I added one other partner to the mix: the United States and its citizens. In every organization I've had the honor to manage, I've created a culture that encourages employees to be patriotic in supporting our democracy and to be generous in supporting those less fortunate. It may sound corny, but I believe a firm takes on the personality of the individual running the show. I'm proud of my patriotism, and I'm proud of my philanthropic activities. I believe that successful corporations as well as individuals should be willing to give something back to our country and to those less fortunate.

This isn't a quid pro quo for the acceptance of selfishness or for using the self-interest of others as a tool. It's simply the right thing to do. I never expected or mandated that my employees replicate my patriotism or philanthropy. However, through leading by example, my firm and its employees were renowned for their patriotic flair and generosity. I believe it all emanates from treating your stakeholder family fairly and caring about people. Employees embrace that culture because they want to be both a contributor to it and a recipient of it.

Of course, while treating your stakeholder family fairly, you can fall into the trap of treating your real family unfairly. I learned that only in hindsight.

All successful, ambitious people are personally selfish to some degree. This goes beyond just the desire to pursue your self-interest in carving up the power and money in business. You can't work the long hours that success requires and can't set the individualistic priorities that ambition dictates without stealing somewhat from your loved ones. Some may think that a selfish perspective is rationalized with the rewards of money and prestige. Perhaps. But what if your loved ones don't really care as much for those material rewards as you do? The truth is that successful people do what they do because they love doing it. The career is their passion, their mistress. It's the adrenaline that drives their metabolism. The drive to spend those long hours working is as essential a part of their genetic makeup as is their DNA.

When I was a young, ambitious manager climbing the ladder at Merrill Lynch, I worked six days a week and practically every night. My first wife and I had been having problems for years, and my focus on the job was certainly one factor in our eventual breakup. After we divorced, my two young daughters spent every weekend with me, and I ended up taking them to work with me on Saturdays. If there was a silver lining to the dissolution of my first marriage, it was that it forced me to spend time with my girls every weekend and on holidays. I'm sure going to daddy's office was not high on the list of what two children wanted to do on their weekend, but at least we were spending time together—more time together, in fact, than when their mother and I were still married. I felt I simply could not refuse any business-related request. It wasn't until much later in my career that I learned people will accommodate your calendar, that you can sometimes say no, and that you can and should prioritize time spent with your family.

Today I still work long hours—but only Monday to Friday. I still have a great many evening appointments, but only from Monday to Thursday. I do not bring a briefcase home on the weekend and rarely allow anyone or anything to intrude on my Saturdays and Sundays at home with my wife. I'm working just as hard as I did then, but now much smarter. My staff adjusts to my calendar, and my secretary manages my appointments to conform to the rhythms of my condensed seventy-hour week.

If you're going to become a successful leader, you need to reconcile yourself to your own selfishness, not just the selfishness of others. Realize that you're going to spend far more time working, and perhaps traveling, than your loved ones would like. Many of your peers will spend more time with their families than you do with yours. And although the material rewards your family gains from all this time working is welcome, it will not compensate for the nights and weekends you're away. Finally, accept that the psychic rewards that come from your ambition and eventual success, while satisfying to you, may mean much less, if anything at all, to your loved ones. This is one of the prices of success. You'll need to sacrifice on the amount of time you spend with your loved ones. Compensate by not sacrificing on the quality of that time.

My early years in management at Merrill Lynch began under fire. I faced the challenges of changing compensation practices, dealing with deregulation, and profitably operating a financial services firm smack in the middle of a bear market. I was thirty-two years old when, in 1980, another crisis engulfed Wall Street.

The Hunt brothers—Nelson Bunker Hunt and William Herbert Hunt, the sons of H. L. Hunt—cornered the silver market and drove prices to unprecedented levels. Silver surpassed forty dollars an ounce, and clients were scrambling to cash in all their silver-denominated coins, such as dimes and quarters. Brokerage firms had no way of knowing at the time that the Hunt brothers had multiple accounts at multiple firms, and their buying frenzy through those multiple accounts drove the silver futures contracts up the limit each day. Commodities futures contract prices are allowed to move up or down a specified amount during each trading day. Once the amount is reached, trades are limited to the maximum move up or down.

The Hunt brothers leveraged their positions by continually using the growing buying power within their margin accounts, which they artificially created by driving silver prices higher. Like any other bubble created in the marketplace by irrational buying, the bubble ultimately burst. Silver prices that had gone up the limit each day began to fall down the limit each day. As futures contracts moved down the limit almost immediately each morning, the Hunt brothers could not sell their positions. The very leverage they created by manipulating prices on the way up now worked against them on the way down. They began receiving margin calls from all of the brokerage firms that had extended them credit. Rumors circulated throughout the brokerage community as to the severity of potential losses if the Hunt brothers could not post additional collateral to meet their margin calls. It was rumored that Bache Securities had taken a $10 million loss, an amount that was considered catastrophic back then.

At the time the crisis hit, I was responsible for margin, commodity, and international operations, and for customer-side processing. Merrill Lynch had a series of accounts not only with the Hunt brothers but with the Hunt sisters as well, so our exposure was significant. Don Regan, Merrill Lynch's chairman and CEO at the time, called for an emergency meeting to be held at the firm's apartment at the Essex House in New York City.

Regan was an ex-Marine colonel who ran the firm with an iron hand. He had an immense command presence, was extraordinarily intelligent, had a quick wit, and was a wonderful extemporaneous speaker. I had been in front of him maybe six times up to that point, and I had no idea what to expect when I was summoned to attend this emergency meeting. Prior to the meeting at the Essex House the next day, I had the presence of mind to send Vic Silano, my head of commodity operations, to London, where the International Commodities Clearing House (ICCH) was located. The ICCH was the depository for silver bullion when the owner of a silver futures contract took delivery of the precious metal. The Hunt brothers had done just that, and they had posted the physical bullion as collateral for the margin accounts with us. I wanted to ensure that every ounce of silver we had as collateral was indeed in possession at the ICCH and that it couldn't be moved to any other firm or location.

When I entered Merrill Lynch's apartment, four other officers, all of them senior to me, were present. Five minutes later Regan entered. He made a profound statement that influenced me for the balance of my career: "We are here to assess our exposure to the Hunt accounts and to seek a solution to minimize the damage. There will be no postmortems—only solutions. We have three hours until Mr. Hunt arrives, at which time we will tell him what, if anything, we are prepared to do going forward." Regan's words, his command presence, and his coolness under fire had more influence on me than any other general or corporate officer had before or has had since.

At around noon, Nelson Bunker Hunt arrived and pleaded his case. He had the audacity to request that Merrill Lynch extend even more credit to him and his brother. We summarily rejected that request. Earlier in the day, I had received confirmation from Vic Silano that our collateral was accounted for and secure. Despite this collateral, the Hunt brothers owed Merrill Lynch approximately $5 million, and their margin calls were growing each day—and not only with us but with every other major firm on the Street. As our meeting reached an impasse, primarily due to Hunt's insistence that we lend him more, I spoke up.

I informed Hunt that as the Merrill Lynch officer in charge of margin lending, I was going to sell out his silver positions the next day unless our margin calls were met with cash or additional collateral. I suggested that absent his ability to post cash, we would accept a cross-collateral guarantee from his sisters' accounts, which were long oil stocks and had no silver positions. As his face turned red, he pushed back from the table, stood up, stared directly at me, and asked, "Young man, do you know who you are talking to?"

I replied, "Yes, sir, and if you would, please leave your gold watch on the table before you leave." To this day, I don't know what prompted me to take such a brash position. But I didn't react well to this oil baron who owed our firm so much money and was trying to bully us into giving him even more of our money to lose, and the situation emboldened me.

The next day we received the cross-collateral from the Hunt sisters. Merrill Lynch was one of the few firms that did not lose any money from the Hunt silver crisis. Beyond just helping the firm avert losses, I also won Don Regan's respect that day. From then on until his departure for government service, he invited me to participate in many of the strategic discussions at the firm.

I received another crowning lesson during the stock market crash of October 1987. Merrill Lynch's success in navigating this crisis can at least partly be attributed to its corporate leaders' understanding that even in the midst of a global economic meltdown, brokers and clients were most concerned with the impact on their individual lives, their careers, and their net worth.

The week of October 12, 1987, began with a litany of bad news. The U.S. trade deficit was expanding to an unhealthy level, tensions between Israel and its neighbors were escalating, and President Reagan and congressional Democrats were at an impasse over the federal budget. Relations between the White House and the Congress were so strained that numerous headlines portrayed our government as being in budget gridlock. On Wednesday, October 14, 1987, the Dow Jones Industrial Average dropped 95.46 points, a new record. It fell another 58 points the next day.

Underlying these geopolitical and budgetary strains was the beginning of a subtle divergence between the stock market and the futures market. A hedging strategy had been embraced by many mega-investment institutions: they tried to offset future gains or losses within their portfolios by buying or selling a corresponding futures contract, giving the holder a future put or call on a fixed price or stock price of a market index, such as the Dow Jones Industrial Average or the Standard & Poor's 500. This investment strategy became known as portfolio insurance.

Unfortunately, as these institutions have so painfully discovered some thirty years later, these strategies are more conceptual than real. As is the case with any other concept, the material assumptions used when forming the concept must remain constant for it to become a reality. Most of the hedging models I've observed throughout my career fail to understand two critical variables. First, the concept assumes that liquidity exists. Without liquidity there is no exit, prices are artificial, and the underlying security and the derivative will divorce each other. And second, if too many asset managers deploy the same hedging strategy, there's no one to hedge against.

In 2008, the demise of mortgage-backed loan portfolios, as well as commercial real estate–backed securities, was directly associated with the same two critical variables: lack of liquidity and an overabundance of hedging strategies. Obviously no one had learned the lessons of the crash of 1987.

In 1987, I was head of the retail branches of Merrill Lynch. As Friday, October 16, approached, negative convergence clouded the skies. (Negative convergence, or nonconvergence, is the failure of futures contracts and the value of their underlying commodities to reach the same value at the time the contracts must be settled. Convergence, or the market's ability to discern the value of a commodity, is the basis of the entire futures market.) On that day the Dow Jones Industrial Average experienced its first triple-digit loss in history, plummeting more than 108 points. Worldwide panic escalated, and every firm on Wall Street scrambled over the weekend to assess its liability, primarily emanating from margin calls.

In response, Merrill Lynch established a war room manned by Bill Schreyer, chairman; Dan Tully, president; John "Launny" Steffens, head of consumer markets; Bob Farrell, our market technician; and myself. We represented a great mix of talent and experience. Bill Schreyer's forte was capital markets and institutional clients. Dan Tully came up through the retail ranks and had been both a branch manager and a divisional manager heading products and services. John "Launny" Steffens was my immediate superior; he came up through the retail ranks and was perhaps the best marketing executive that Wall Street had ever produced. I was running the sales force and had firsthand experience running customer-side operations such as margin, international, and commodities.

And Bob Farrell was the most highly regarded technical analyst on the street.

On Monday, October 19, the market fell 508 points, trading 604 million shares. That volume was three times greater than any previous trading day in the history of the New York Stock Exchange. The blood now began flowing down Wall Street. Clients who had borrowed on margin were immediately subjected to a call for additional capital or they would be sold out. Many of our competitors would not allow their clients any time to react by insisting that their margin call had to be met within twenty-four hours. Several discount firms would not even answer their telephones. Merrill Lynch chose a solution-oriented approach, communicating to our brokers and, through them, to our clients.

We had the advantage of having recently installed a direct broadcast system (DBS) that allowed management to communicate to our more than five hundred offices live using a television hookup. Throughout the day, we used this system to keep the financial advisors abreast of the market conditions and how we wanted our clients handled. Our frequent communications with the field had a discernible stabilizing effect despite the fact that none of us had dealt with a market crash of this magnitude before. It was an important lesson about the importance of frequent and high-level communications with constituents during a crisis. Several firms overreacted and created such a degree of ill will that Merrill Lynch ultimately gained market share at their expense.

On Tuesday, October 20, the market opened up 200 points, but by 12:30 P.M., it was down 100 points. The cash market and the forward market were totally disconnected. The

Dow stood on a cash basis of 1700, whereas on the futures market, it was quoted at 1300. No one knew if this unusual 400-point difference between cash value and expectations represented the eye of the storm. I vividly recall asking Bob Farrell what he thought was going to happen next. Misty-eyed, he replied, "Joe, I have never seen anything like this."

The management of the New York Stock Exchange signaled that they were considering closing the exchange. The financial world as we understood it was on the brink of collapse.

I was not then, and am not now, privy to what actions the senior managers of our competitors were taking on that Tuesday. But I was proud then, and continue to be proud now, of the actions of the team heading up Merrill Lynch, the world's largest investment firm at the time. Bill Schreyer called the White House and forcefully suggested that President Reagan agree to a compromise with the congressional Democrats. Dan Tully insisted that the New York Stock Exchange not close, as that would shatter market confidence around the world. John "Launny" Steffens and I provided guidance to our financial advisors and the firm's clients, reassuring them that their interests were our primary concerns. Before that Tuesday ended, a day actually much scarier than the now-infamous Black Monday, the dangerous disconnect between the cash and futures market eased. J.P. Morgan, whose stock fell from $40 to $30 a share, commenced a corporate buyback, which was emulated by several other corporations. The New York Stock Exchange remained open. On Wednesday, October 21, the so-called smart money started buying stocks.

There's no way that the kind of crisis communication the Merrill Lynch management team engaged in would have worked by e-mail. Don't allow advances in information and communication technology fool you into believing that you can take the pulse, or push a touch point, of your employees or clients without actual human contact. Although you may be able to achieve a higher multiple of productivity through the use of Internet technology, you cannot lead using e-mail, especially during a crisis.

Technology is depersonalizing society in general and business in particular, I believe to the detriment of both. People today text-message or e-mail rather than speak or meet. That loss of human contact eliminates a vital opportunity to discern nuance, intuit motivation, and get a reading on confidence and satisfaction.

Parenthetically, reliance on information technology can also result in intimate private conversations and exchanges becoming part of the permanent record, without their being able to be placed in any context or explained. A private joke embedded in an e-mail doesn't end with a "ha-ha." Its meaning is open to interpretation by a litigious attorney for the next seven years. It's no coincidence that most of the corporate scandals of the past decade were adjudicated based on voluminous records of electronic communications.

Subsequent to the crash, Merrill Lynch held an all-managers meeting in Chicago. At the meeting I unveiled a videotape that articulated our strategy going forward. I had written the script during a lengthy plane trip. I was the only speaker on the tape, and all office managers were to present the tape to their respective offices when they returned from the meeting.

My words articulated an understanding and empathy for what our clients, financial advisors, and managers had just experienced. I insisted that they, as managers and brokers, had to appreciate and sympathize with the tremendous losses our clients had just endured. But in no way were they to assume guilt. The markets are not in our control, I told them, but providing appropriate advice and counsel, during any market condition, is in our control. It is our obligation. I proceeded to give them a strategy, a road map, or perhaps better stated, a protocol for hope, for their clients as well as for themselves. It turned out to be the right message at the right time, as it gave our office managers a direction that none of their competitors had.

Because of my meteoric climb in the firm and my being lauded for my marketing work by industry observers, my name was already being bandied about as a possible future leader of the firm. After the tape played, the managers gave it a standing ovation that lasted ten minutes. In hindsight, I believe it was largely because the managers could see that someone in New York "had their back." At least part of that response was also, I think, thanks in recognition of my role in looking out for the interests of the brokers and their clients during the crisis we'd just survived. While the managers were still applauding, a senior manager ran up to me shouting, "Joe, you are going to be our next president." I responded by thanking him and telling him that I sincerely doubted it: "You clapped too long, too loud, and too soon."

I was right in predicting I'd never become president of Merrill Lynch. But it wouldn't be because I was getting too much attention or acclaim.

"There's nobody else at your left, at your right, or at your back, that you want than Joe Grano."

—DAN TULLY, FORMER CHAIRMAN
AND CEO OF MERRILL LYNCH

Chapter Five

YOU CAN'T
PREDICT A HERO

One of the realities of combat is that you can't predict a hero. Take, for instance, the well-documented heroism of Sergeant Alvin York in World War I who, after having his application for conscientious objector status rejected, went on to win the Medal of Honor. Or Audie Murphy in World War II, who became one of America's most highly decorated soldiers despite being so short and slight that commanders repeatedly tried to keep him out of combat. Both are excellent examples of two unassuming individuals who unexpectedly rose above and beyond their fellow soldiers in response to a crisis.

Heroism is not measured by physical stature or oral bravado. You can't anticipate what your reaction or someone else's will be when bullets are flying and people are seeking to cause you bodily harm. My experiences in combat taught me that at times, the biggest, baddest, loudest bully types were often the first to cower when "the shit hit the fan."

I am not suggesting the fear of combat isn't universal. Quite the contrary, every soldier I ever led in battle entered the fray with some fear and apprehension. I was no different. When the reality of the situation is accepted by your brain, there are three natural responses: you hide, you proceed with caution, or your adrenaline overcomes the fear and you move to eradicate the danger.

My men would all join me on patrol with an unspoken wish that we not encounter the enemy. However, when such encounters did occur, one of the most difficult parts of my job as a commander was to calm down those with a proclivity to take unnecessary and potentially deadly risks: to play John Wayne. The adrenaline generated in those potential heroes sometimes needed to be tempered, as their instincts were not always in tune with the dangers in front of them. There were times when discretion truly was the better part of valor. Of course, there were other times when those very heroic instincts were what saved the day for all.

If there is any significant positive that actual combat delivers, it's that it forces the battlefield commander to instantaneously process whatever information is available. To this day I'm capable of processing vast amounts of information quickly and honing in on the core issues relevant to the situation. I believe that my ability to ignore the minutiae and respond quickly was shaped by my experiences in combat. And it's crucial that the person in charge is clear that the value of human life is always greater than the dollar value of money: I was never concerned with spending a million dollars of artillery or air support if it would save one life.

Fear isn't confined to combat or other situations that threaten physical harm. I learned that when people are facing a financial or business bullet, their reaction is as unpredictable as it is for those facing live fire. You can never predict what the reaction will be of people facing a business catastrophe. Some coworker you might have suspected would throw you under the bus when, for example, a major client sues, will stand alongside you and face the peril, whatever its cost. Others you believed were your truest allies in the office may abandon you at the first hint of trouble.

I experienced the unpredictability of heroism in financial situations firsthand. People I believed would stand up for their financial obligations, or I believed had the integrity to be trustee of my estate, cowered and hid when confronted with a financial crisis. As a result, I found myself going down in a personal ball of flames.

In 1982 I was a senior marketing executive at Merrill Lynch. As a side venture with a small group of fellow businessmen, I created a general partnership to build and operate a condo-hotel and ski resort in Ascutney, Vermont. Based on the then prevailing tax code, we devised a model in which investors would purchase a condo as part of a condo-hotel. Each owner could personally use his or her own condo two weeks out of the year, and for the remaining fifty weeks the condo would be pooled with ninety-nine others and rented as a hotel unit. Above and beyond a unit within the condo-hotel, the investor owned a percentage of an adjoining ski resort and would also participate in potential real estate profits from future development at the resort.

It was a wonderful concept, considering that at the time, investors would have received up to two dollars of tax write-off for every one dollar invested. We raised $84 million, built the hundred-unit condo-hotel, and revitalized the bankrupt ski resort with new lifts, trails, and snowmaking equipment, as well as a new lodge. We even bought the local town a brand-new fire truck to service the resort and surrounding community.

My partners in this venture were a self-made entrepreneur; a highly successful manager at Merrill Lynch; that manager's accountant; and my boss, the president of Merrill Lynch, who eventually became the firm's chairman. For the first four years, I directed the operation, got the facilities built, and physically worked there every weekend. In 1985 I was promoted to take charge of Merrill Lynch's vast array of offices and stock-brokers, and as a result I couldn't continue to run the operation at the resort. My position was assumed by the partner who was an accountant.

The following year, President Reagan changed the federal tax law and crushed real estate projects throughout the country. We had $16 million of debt on the project and still had approximately twenty-seven condos left unsold. Due to the tax change, people stopped buying vacation homes because there was now no interest deductibility for second-home mortgages. We weren't the only ones in trouble. Major developers such as Donald Trump and Reichman Real Estate were also experiencing difficulties within their real estate empires. My partners and I were not personally liable for the $16 million in debt, but we were in the middle of arranging financing for the next phase of the development. Despite the precarious environment, we still felt confident in the long-term potential of the resort.

The accountant partner introduced the rest of us to an executive representing a highly regarded global banking institution, who suggested we consolidate all current and future funding with his institution as lead bank. His bank arranged a refinance of our existing loan and an additional $11 million for the next phase of development. This new bank, which served as lead lender, was joined in the financing by another foreign bank, as well as our original bank in Vermont. Based on approval of the new loan package, we made multiple commitments to vendors and started the next phase of development.

Two weeks prior to the closing of the financial package, the lead bank informed us that the other foreign bank within the lending consortium had backed out of U.S. lending and, hence, out of our project. The lead bank assured us, however, that within a matter of weeks, the missing foreign bank would be replaced. However, to close on the new credit facility, the general partners would have to joint and severally guarantee the original $16 million. (Simply put, signing joint and severally means that individual partners can be held liable for the entire debt regardless of their individual share of the liability.) We were told this would be only temporary until a new lender came aboard. We partners were now effectively boxed in. The project could not fulfill its current obligations, and we could not access the funding without agreeing to this temporary guarantee. We had no choice.

I always believed I was the pauper of the group of partners, because at that time in my career, I had not earned much money. My career was accelerating, but in the 1980s, no one earned the levels of compensation enjoyed in the late 1990s. I also knew that my boss, the president of Merrill Lynch, had the deepest pockets and would be the most at risk if he signed the joint and several guarantee. The lead bank continued to reassure us that the guarantees were temporary. I met my boss at an airport and assured him he would never have to reach into his pocket. Relying on the bank's reputation, we all signed the joint and several guarantee.

Two weeks after the closing of the new credit facility, the lead bank announced that it would also be closing down its operations in the U.S. due to the poor economic environment we were then experiencing. We partners were trapped. What banking institution was going to take the principal investors or partners off the hook when the lead bank had given up on lending in our country? We had no choice but to sue the lead bank for misrepresentation. Of course, in response, the bank called in the loan of $16 million. An expensive legal action ensued and continued for the next three years. We were forced to put the project in bankruptcy. I knew we were in the right and believed we would eventually win the case. What I did not anticipate were the actions of two of my four partners.

During the discovery process, our attorneys uncovered an internal memo sent from the headquarters of the lead bank to its U.S. branch announcing the bank's plan to shut down its U.S. operation. The memo cautioned the U.S. branch not to inform its clients of the impending move, as management wished to preclude a "run on the bank." The memo was dated one month before we were asked to sign our guarantees. Point, set, and match: we win our case—or so I thought.

The lead bank fired its legal representative and hired the former attorney general of the state of Vermont to represent it. He took a different approach to the case, choosing to focus on the general partners individually. What resulted was an allegation that two of my partners had submitted false and misleading financial statements. The bank then adjusted its counterclaims to include bank fraud. As it turned out, the allegation had sufficient merit to put us in danger of losing, due to what you might call two "rotten apples." The three other partners stood to be "contaminated" by the two who had allegedly committed bank fraud. The project had already entered into bankruptcy proceedings, and I was personally keeping the resort open with my own money with the blessing of the bankruptcy court. I also was burdened with the prospect of having to pay my pro-rata share of the $16 million, never mind my promise to my boss that he would never have to reach into his pocket. It got worse.

One of the "rotten apples" declared bankruptcy. The other moved his assets out of his name in order to become judgment proof. A third partner declared personal bankruptcy, leaving just me and my boss. Many nights I stared in the face of my financial bullet as my heart raced with palpitations. My wife had a growing concern for my health, although I never let her know the severity of the situation. Concurrently my boss was about to be promoted to the chairmanship of Merrill Lynch. The last thing he needed was a financial scandal.

I was in one of the top ten managerial positions at Merrill Lynch at the time. I had enjoyed a meteoric rise through the ranks and was a member of the firm's executive committee. On multiple occasions, I was solicited by competitive firms to be their president or take on some other senior position. Despite the appeal of a more senior position and offers of signing bonuses in the millions of dollars, I had always declined. I loved Merrill Lynch and was grateful for all the opportunities it had given me as a disabled veteran. Now I found myself in a position in which I might cost my dear friend and boss the chairmanship of a great firm, cost him $16 million based on my request, and also bring financial ruin to my own family.

My attorneys recommended that I declare bankruptcy. Instead I accepted the presidency of PaineWebber's retail division, along with a $4 million signing bonus. The general counsel at PaineWebber agreed with my attorneys that I should declare bankruptcy. He said to me that the banks could go to hell and that a year later, no one would care that I'd declared bankruptcy. I told *him* to go to hell because a year later *I* would care. It was about my reputation, my signature on the guarantee, and my word to a friend. I arranged for an additional $4 million loan from a major bank. I then went to the banks that were owed the $16 million and offered a payment schedule to pay them back in full, as long as they charged no interest, let my boss off the hook, and agreed to drop all claims. They accepted. Five years later, they were paid off in full. I resolved to never again sign joint and severally.

The consequences of my decision to face the music, so to speak, were primarily favorable. I was never sued by any investor as they watched me do everything in my power to keep the project alive. I would go on to even greater heights at PaineWebber, achieving the chairman and CEO seat. This allowed me to earn back the money I had lost. My friend and former boss became one of the best chairmen in Merrill Lynch's history. Neither he nor the firm suffered any embarrassment from the failed project. Most important, I had kept my word.

On the negative side, I probably aged ten years from the experience. I had to leave a firm I loved. My boss, friend, and mentor felt betrayed when I left Merrill Lynch because I never told him the real reason why. I kept the truth from him because I knew that he would have put his own future at Merrill Lynch at risk rather than let me take the bullet for the Ascutney disaster. We didn't speak for seven years. I waited until he retired and then wrote him a letter explaining my actions and why I would never betray his trust in me. The next time I saw him, he had tears in his eyes as he hugged me and said, "I should have known."

If every partner in the Ascutney project had faced the financial bullets, the cost would have been $3.2 million each—painful but certainly recoverable for individuals with the kind of resources each possessed. But as I came to learn, whether it's on the battlefield or in business, you can't predict a hero.

I grew up in a culture that dictated that your word was your bond. We consummated a deal or a contract with a handshake and a verbal commitment. We honored both no less solemnly than a signed contract. However, since my idyllic, or perhaps naive, youth, I've learned that you cannot assume that all of the individuals shaking your hand or giving you their word share your culture or, conveniently perhaps, won't forget your shared culture when they are facing dire circumstances.

In today's society, you're compelled to conduct a background check on a prospective business partner. You're also forced to engage a litany of attorneys to construct a contract, since a handshake has no bearing in the current sea of litigiousness. It is, frankly, depressing to me to have too often experienced a situation in which someone reneged on an agreement after giving me his or her word and a handshake.

My fear is that this now common failure to stand by a handshake or verbal agreement is indicative of a deterioration of the value system that originally defined our democracy. We began as a nation in which men actually fought duels over matters of principle and in which the worst thing you could say of someone else was that he was not honorable. We thankfully abandoned dueling, yet for generations maintained a sense that a man's word was his bond. Promises, both overt and inferred, were never taken lightly. Today we seem all too quick to both promise and renege. If you look at the demise of historically dominant empires such as Rome or Persia, you find that one common denominator is the breakdown of their values. I hope we don't become yet another example.

I sometimes wonder if affluence begets arrogance, and arrogance begets self-indulgence. Whenever employees or research analysts ask me what can go wrong in today's successful organization, I respond, "We can't allow ourselves to become arrogant." I certainly want my employees to attain a successful, self-confident swagger, but never at the expense of the highest levels of integrity and sensitivity toward others, including our competitors.

I believe the way you treat competitors is as indicative of your firm's character and values as the way you treat your constituents. I always respected my competitors when I was at Merrill Lynch and later at PaineWebber. Of course, I enjoyed outperforming them any time I could, but never with a view that I wanted to crush them or put them out of business. The demise or problems of a major competitor are a reflection of your whole industry. A major oil spill from an oil producer, for instance, taints the image of the oil industry as a whole. When a financial firm goes bankrupt, clients of all firms become concerned with the safety of their assets.

On several occasions, I instructed my management teams to present a new, in-house, state-of-the-art compliance system to our regulators, such as the Securities and Exchange Commission, with instructions that the regulator could suggest to any competitive firm in need of assistance that we would give them the technology. There's no question such a decision could have made a weak competitor stronger. However, such a decision also made our industry stronger, which ultimately helped my firm succeed due to a more vibrant environment.

An ancillary benefit was that we created goodwill with our regulators. Every firm faces some regulatory action in its business cycle. Whether the regulators believe the infractions were intended or due to an honest oversight can mean the difference between a slap on the hand or a multimillion-dollar fine. That determination begins with the regulator's perception of your firm and its management team. Are you perceived as the good guys or as the bad guys always pushing the envelope? Good healthy competition and good collaborative regulation serve to make your firm even better.

To succeed in business doesn't require the bravery of a Sergeant York or an Audie Murphy. There are many individuals who have achieved great wealth without having great integrity. But to be a consistent leader, to win the willing support of others in crises time after time, you must have the bravery of your convictions. A winning leader honors commitments to peers, shareholders, employees, customers, and competitors too, even when it might not be convenient.

"Joe Grano brings an energy, a passion, a commitment, and a can-do attitude to absolutely everything he undertakes. I call that leadership. That's why the president chose him to chair his Homeland Security Advisory Council."

—GOVERNOR TOM RIDGE, FORMER SECRETARY FOR THE U.S. DEPARTMENT OF HOMELAND SECURITY

Chapter Six

THE TRUTH IS NEVER WRONG

Facts are sometimes hard to accept. Most people are uneasy about change, even in a crisis, and they are uncomfortable with the new until convinced that it is better than the old. When you're facing a crisis and you predicate a change in policy, strategy, or direction based on facts or the truth, your constituents will be more likely to embrace a new approach if you begin with an honest assessment of the situation, followed by an open dialogue that articulates the facts. End with a well-thought-out action plan that assigns responsibilities and establishes measurement standards. Another important tenet of good management is, "What is measured, gets done."

If you are a new manager or have been given a new assignment, take sixty to ninety days to listen and assess the situation, gather the facts, learn the culture, and evaluate the management. Then, and only then, design your strategy and operating plan. If you don't take this time to learn, listen, evaluate, and construct your plan, you run the risk of destroying inherent value and alienating your employees.

Any executive propagating major changes in strategy or culture must be sensitive to the legacies of the business, the management team, the internal processes, and the existing pay practices. There are two additional important tenets you must accept and plan for prior to initiating your action plan. First, you cannot change culture quickly. In fact, the only accelerators of cultural change are pain and agony. Second, remember that people ultimately always do what they are paid to do; hence, you must change compensation to be in direct support of the changes in activity you are requesting from your employees.

Once you have identified the problems, formatted a solution, communicated your plans and strategies, and have commensurably aligned your compensation practices, everyone will be rowing in the same direction. Then you can cry out, "Ramming speed!"

I arrived at PaineWebber in February 1988, taking the job of president of consumer markets. From my perch at Merrill Lynch, I never considered PaineWebber a serious competitor. After arriving and spending ninety days gathering the facts and assessing the firm, I came to understand why: there wasn't much to compete against.

PaineWebber at the time was the least productive of the seven largest brokerage firms. The firm had the lowest amount of client assets per broker, which not only resulted in low productivity but also contributed to a horrific compliance profile indicating instances of inappropriate conduct. Those low asset levels were churned, or overly traded, to generate commissions. The demographic profile of the brokers looked like a goalpost. At one end was an overconcentration of young brokers in the business for less than three years. At the opposite end were many with a length of service over ten years. And literally no one was in between the posts. The firm enjoyed a credible institutional equity business but had little to no footing in investment banking. PaineWebber's research division was excellent; however, neither the retail nor institutional side of the firm was doing enough business to pay for it. The culture on the retail side could best be described as "lowest-cost-centric": PaineWebber had the lowest-paid sales assistants and managers among the major competitors. The culture on the capital markets side of the firm was "hot-dot-centric": PaineWebber had highly paid traders and bankers whose earnings were based on "what did you do for me today" scenarios. On both sides of the firm, the prima donnas rather than management ruled.

The firm's chairman, Don Marron, was without question one of the most brilliant people I had ever encountered. He was responsible for his firm surviving under conditions in which many others folded. However, he was not a designer and operator of a consistent business model. To his credit, he gave me the support and authority to move the firm in another direction.

To exacerbate the situation, just before I arrived, the management team in charge of the retail side had attempted to reduce the compensation levels paid to the brokers. I use the word *attempted* because the reaction of PaineWebber's sales force was so negative that management was forced to withdraw the new plan. Ouch!

As you can imagine, the firm was also experiencing an inordinately high turnover rate of brokers who were leaving in droves to join the competition. My constituents who remained were fearful that their new, high-profile president was going to

"Merrill Lynchize" the place, Merrill Lynch having at that time the reputation of a robotic society, as opposed to the gunslinging streets of PaineWebber City.

What had I gotten myself into? The truth is never wrong, and it had led me to a two-word assessment: "Oh shit." If I had known all that was soon coming, the sentiment would have been even stronger.

During my first month at PaineWebber, the over-the-counter department, which sells securities not traded on the New York Stock Exchange and more commonly known as OTC stocks, had a spot secondary offering to our clients of a particular security. (A spot secondary offering is the offer of stock shares for sale, without any additional filings to the Securities and Exchange Commission, made by a company that has already made its initial public offering. Generally the company uses these to raise funds quickly for growth or to refinance.) The stock was sold to clients at a price of around seven dollars a share.

At PaineWebber there was a Chinese wall between trading desks and the research department. A trader was, of necessity, aware of what our research analysts thought of a security. They were not privy, however, to what a future change of opinion might be so that they couldn't trade in advance on inside information.

Sure enough, the day after the offering, our own research division issued a sell recommendation on the stock we sold to our clients the previous day with an exuberant buy recommendation. Technically we did nothing wrong. The system worked as it should have. However, our clients were looking at approximately $2 million in losses in a single day. Our financial advisors were totally embarrassed.

Neither the clients nor the financial advisors cared about the rationale for the Chinese wall. They all felt that they had been misled. My general counsel and the president of the entire firm concluded that since we had done nothing technically wrong, there was no reason to take any action to ameliorate the situation. If we did, they said, we'd be opening a Pandora's box.

I landed on the other side. I told them that this was not an issue of technicalities or of a Pandora's box. It was about perception and goodwill. The truth, as our clients and brokers perceived it, was that we had let them both down. Yes, it was actually an unfortunate coincidence. But I believed that the credibility of our financial advisers and the firm were at stake. I said that when you have a turd, don't nibble on it, swallow it.

The expression, which I believe comes from the Deep South, refers to taking a bold action immediately when confronted with a problem. In the financial services industry, it is particularly germane when you have a bad trade or error. Too often a trader will want to trade out of a bad call or an office manager will seek a way around a trade made in error. Actually they are always better off facing the music by getting out of the bad situation and taking their losses. I have seen bad trades grow much worse when individuals don't "swallow them" and instead choose to "nibble" at the problem.

When the president and the general counsel instructed me to take no action, I said that they might as well give away their $27 million advertising budget and look for a replacement for me if they didn't bust (that is, cancel) the trade. I've always believed that while a satisfied customer talks to one person, a dissatisfied customer talks to thirteen. As they stood there in silence, I picked up the phone and instructed our OTC department to bust the trade and make our clients whole. They were to charge my organization for the $2 million loss.

Was I setting an unhealthy precedent? Perhaps. But in my twenty years in the business, such an acute coincidence had never happened to me before. (And in all the years since, I've never seen it happen again.) Could I have legally defended the trade? Absolutely. But was this about legality or morality? Perceptively we could not defend the morality of what had transpired; we couldn't overcome our clients' and brokers' perceptions of the truth. I believe the decision was good not just for our clients and advisors but for our shareholders as well. I took the $2 million dollar loss to make our clients whole and to protect the reputation of our financial advisors and our firm. Many lawyers and corporate presidents would opt for the legal or technical position, but there are times you need to opt for the people involved. My actions certainly sent a message to the people at PaineWebber that things were going to change.

My goal was to turn PaineWebber into an organization that was client-centric and solution based, understanding that our employees were clients too. By being client-centric, we could maintain a pulse on the current and future acceptability of our firm's value proposition. A good salesperson can provide more timely and accurate information relative to client demand than any academic exercise conducted at corporate headquarters.

I spent the rest of my first sixty days at PaineWebber getting to know my management team and evaluating the firm's profile, market position, strengths, and weaknesses, as well as the value proposition, product by product, and market by market. It was a month-long effort to uncover the facts and learn the truth about the organization's position. At the end of the investigations, I could only conclude that we had a very broken franchise. In 1987, the year before I arrived, the retail side of the firm reported a loss of $96 million.

When an organization is not performing well, the subsequent decline in stock price, the obvious dissatisfaction of clients, and the lower compensation earned by employees constitute the pain and agony needed to institute rapid change. Given our situation at PaineWebber, we could move quickly to change the business model as well as the culture because all our constituents wanted to end their suffering.

Three of my past associates at Merrill Lynch asked if they could join me at PaineWebber: Bob Silver, who became my chief administrative officer; Vic Silano, who headed commodity operations at Merrill Lynch; and John Puccio, who ran the back office for stock loans. Of the three, only Bob Silver came as a direct report to me.

Together, Bob Silver and I spent days 60 to 90 at PaineWebber categorizing the good, the bad, and the ugly. We created a series of strategies and tactics to fix the bad and dissolve the ugly. I announced a new management team out in the field and within the home office. Approximately ten of forty positions changed. I did not want to get rid of people simply because they were from the previous regime. Only one of the ten new people who filled positions was hired externally; the remaining nine were promoted from within the firm. Fortunately, one of them was a young man named Mark Sutton whom I moved from the field to the home office. He ultimately became my president, as well as my replacement when I left the firm.

I kept so many individuals from the previous regime because by then, I had witnessed too many new CEOs take the helm of a firm and, because of their desire to put their own legacy moniker on the organization, destroy intrinsic value. New CEOs have a tendency to discard many, if not most, of the qualified old guard managers to make room for their new, perceived loyal managers who "get it." At some point in their lives, I believe, these CEOs must have read Machiavelli's *The Prince* and have chosen to interpret it literally and live by its principles. Ultimately the failure to earn the loyalty of subordinates, the unwillingness to align inherited as well as new talent commensurately with the tasks at hand, and the lack of appreciation for the contributory components of the culture that need to be protected, results in the prince becoming a pauper. Real leaders do not mandate or design adherence to their point of view. Quite the contrary, they seek disparate opinions and earn the willing obedience of their subordinates.

I developed a job charter for each position in the hierarchy, laid out the goals, and changed the compensation to support the new strategy and structure. We created a pro forma for the new strategy for the next five years and drafted an underlying business plan for the next three years. For the first year, we had a stated goal of reducing the 1987 loss of $96 million to a loss of $36 million, for a $60 million improvement. I secretly had a goal of earning a profit, even if it was only one dollar.

I have always managed using this five-year/three-year formula. The business plan needs to be flexible and can be finetuned month to month, given environmental or unforeseen consequences. Changes to the strategy, however, require the equivalent of an act of God. The management team, as well as all the employees, are walked through both. They are told what I expect from the business plan, as well as from the five-year strategy. I do pro forma projections of both and articulate how results will be measured and how employees will share in the firm's eventual success.

Ninety days after my arrival, I brought every manager in the organization to a weekend meeting in Dallas. I presented the profile of the firm, the areas needing improvement, and a tactical and strategic plan spelling out the ten initiatives needed to achieve our goals.

I knew I needed to get my managers on board because we were fighting a captain's war—one that would be won in the field. When you manage a decentralized organization with geographically dispersed points of sale, you must rely heavily on your office managers, or "captains." They are the motivators and educators of the salespeople. Their demeanor and professionalism have more influence on the perceived quality of the brand than any advertising campaign. The experience that a client has at a local point of sale formulates that client's perception of your firm.

With encouragement, many managers spoke up with a common message: ten initiatives were too many for the management team to absorb in one year. I explained that by aligning compensation with the activity we desired, we would effectively institutionalize five of the ten changes we were seeking. Employees would be eager to adopt and execute our action plan since that would help them earn their living. I told the managers they needed to simply support those five while leading the remaining five.

We called the plan The Perfect Ten. Here were its elements:

- Role of management
- Asset gathering
- Productivity
- Physical distribution
- Fee-based revenue
- Cost of distribution
- Recruiting
- Management recruiting
- Retention
- Training

This Perfect Ten was our strategic response to the risks and opportunities uncovered during our environmental assessment of the firm and the industry as a whole. We created both a five- and a three-year pro forma for each initiative: the five-year model to support and justify the strategic plan and the three-year model to support the underlying business plan. We consolidated the pro formas for the ten initiatives so the team could see firsthand the power of a coordinated plan that could move PaineWebber from a losing enterprise to a winner.

By sharing with the total management team our environmental assessment of PaineWebber and the industry as a whole, we established a baseline for what I called "truth and consequences": every member of the management team learned the truth and became acutely aware of the consequences if we didn't move to ameliorate the situation.

We exceeded my private goal of earning $1 in the first year by $12,999,999. Our $13 million in earnings, coming a year after a loss of $96 million, represented a turnaround of approximately $109 million in one year. We subsequently sustained our momentum by moving from last to first in productivity per financial advisor, moving from last to first in assets per financial advisor, and moving from last to first in attracting financial advisors from competitors. In 2000, when PaineWebber merged with UBS, the retail group was earning $600 million.

Due in large part to the massive turnaround in consumer markets, I was promoted in 1994 to president of the entire firm. This position added the responsibilities for investment banking, equity and fixed income sales and trading, research, and asset management. Collectively in that year, these capital market entities were losing approximately $250 million.

The negative influences peppered throughout these organizations were the result of a siloed, hot-dot-centric culture reinforced by several prima donnas within each silo. A piece of business, a hot trader, a high-profile investment banker, or an institutionally ranked researched analyst dictated the firm's resource allocations and dominated the bonus pools. There was no cohesive strategy. It was just "follow the hot dot" and respond to any and all demands from one of the prima donnas.

In my opinion, it was right around this time (mid-1990s) when Wall Street began to lose its perspective relative to pay practices. Leading bankers and research analysts, who were earning $1 million to $3 million a year, were receiving offers from competitors to leave for annual pay packages as high as $15 million. These large bulge bracket Wall Street firms abandoned good management pay practices and adopted a "buy market share at any price" model. No consideration was given to the impact on longer-term costs or the natural escalation of compensation at every level of the organization, as all ships rise with the tide.

After my sixty-day review of the people and the businesses, I concluded that our first priority was to stop the bleeding and ensure that no business activity could result in a loss that would exacerbate the situation. I replaced the heads of investment banking, institutional sales and trading, as well as the asset management company, all through internal promotions. With the new team, we deployed a much more focused strategy, which can be simply described as moving from "being all things to all people" to "being all things to some people." This strategy was supplemented by a series of tactics that forced a new cost discipline across the capital markets organizations and propagated an integrated approach toward the clients we chose to serve. Our blueprint for success had these elements:

- Reducing the number of industries followed within investment banking from fifteen to seven.

- Realigning our research to be in direct support of each of the seven industries.

- Disallowing any direct bonuses from an investment banker, or from an investment banking transaction, directly to a research analyst. All bonus-related funds entered a blind pool and were weighted based primarily on the results of a research analyst's recommendations: buy, okay to buy, hold, or sell.

- Disallowing investment banking from underwriting a security unless the company or security was followed by research and only if the research opinion was rated a hold, okay to buy, or buy.

- Stressing all proprietary positions on every trading desk in the world to ensure no desk could lose more than $25 million in a meltdown. (This was later changed to $50 million as we became profitable.)

- Reviewing all positions on all desks daily (my risk management team and I did this). Each Monday morning, all traders would meet with me to discuss trends in the equity and fixed income markets. A consensus profile would be established for the week and reviewed daily.

- Replying, when approached by a prima donna seeking more compensation along with a threat to leave for a competitor, "Don't let the door hit you in the ass on the way out."

- Realigning the capital committed to the equity trading desk, ensuring our capital supported companies represented by our investment banking companies and equities that our research was recommending.

- Having the entire senior management team visit our major institutional clients to reinforce our integrated strategy in support of their respective businesses.

- Instituting a preferred vendor program that gave higher visibility to asset managers who passed our due diligence and provided higher-quality returns to our clients. We, for example, removed one of our own mutual funds from preferred status when the fund's senior portfolio manager left the firm. We also refused to send order flow to Bernie Madoff's trading firm, despite the revenues we would receive from it. I believed at the time that its operation was having a negative impact on the quality of the equity markets.

- Most important, facilitating an integration of the capital markets and consumer markets management teams by hosting a weekly management meeting with approximately twenty managers from each side of the firm. A hypothetical client was placed at the center of our large conference table, and the managers of both sides of the firm discussed how we could better serve that client. At times I made our hypothetical client a retail broker or an institutional salesperson. This process drove us to a one-firm, client-centric enterprise and had more influence on our ability to out-execute our competitors than any other activity, tactic, or strategy.

When we merged PaineWebber with UBS in 2000, the capital markets organizations matched the consumer markets' contribution of earning $600 million pretax. Together, PaineWebber was earning $1.2 billion before taxes. When I look back at the $96 million loss within consumer markets and the $250 million in losses within the capital markets, I can only reflect on the contributions and sacrifices shared by the dedicated employees and managers of the firm.

The recipe for this turnaround began with learning the facts and sharing the truth. Its execution succeeded by providing solutions to the problems we faced, providing the optimism and aspiration our employees craved, structuring our compensation in direct support of our strategy, and putting in place a management team of whom I could not have been more proud.

I still recall that back in 1988, during the question-and-answer period at that first management meeting in Dallas, one of our better managers, who headed the Portland, Oregon, office, raised his hand and asked me, "When will you know that we have fixed the firm?"

I told him the truth: "You will tell me."

"If you are in a foxhole, there is nobody in the world you would rather have watching your back than Joe Grano. He's not a patsy. He's a tough boss. But his first instinct is to protect his troops."

—STEVE BAUM, FORMER HEAD OF
CAPITAL MARKETS FOR PAINEWEBBER

Chapter Seven

HUMANITY IS MORE IMPORTANT THAN HIERARCHY

Too many executives start believing their own bullshit when they reach the corner office. They fall into the trap of thinking the position they hold is more important than the function they perform. They forget the skills that got them to the top as the position begins to overtake their persona. They stop taking the pulse of their company and worrying about the secretary or the supervisor, and start worrying about appearances and wanting to rub elbows with "the right people." These aren't good leaders.

Failing to realize that their firm's assets ride up and down the elevators, these imperious executives are often unable to anticipate looming crises and are generally ineffective in confronting and overcoming them. Treating others with respect is more than a management technique. It is an extension of your persona rather than an extension of your position as leader, manager, or CEO. It defines you as a caring, approachable, grateful person. When the lobby guard occasionally poked his head into my office at PaineWebber, with no fear in his eyes and a cup of coffee in his hand, and said to me, "Mr. G, I thought you might like a cup of coffee," I knew I was still the same person I was before becoming a CEO.

Throughout this book, I've been offering suggestions and examples based on my own experiences as a leader in military, corporate, and community environments. These best practices and interpersonal skills can be learned and can go a long way in positioning you as a good leader in times of crisis. But none of these practices or skills, and no amount of mentorship or advice, however well intentioned or practical, can substitute for one core quality: having respect and caring for the individuals you employ or manage, particularly in times of crisis. No trade secrets or best practices can take the place of treating your fellow human beings, whatever their status in an organization's hierarchy, as valuable and important individuals who are worthy of consideration.

Our actions ultimately shape the perceptions that our subordinates and peers have of us. A leader at any level must reflect that respect and care for the individual. Your subordinates understand and expect to be measured by employee performance. They know they're part of a business and that the bottom line matters. However, they also crave a boss and a culture that appreciates them as individuals. That craving becomes ravenous in times of crisis, when the odds are that they will feel insecure and perhaps even helpless. Whether the crisis leads the rank-and-file to fear for their financial or their physical safety, they need a leader whom they believe understands their fears and will address their needs as human beings, not just as cogs in the organizational machine. Employees want to know that you realize they aren't just lines on a profit-and-loss statement. They want to know you recognize their essential humanity.

Before I became a high-level corporate executive I never would have believed it necessary to spell this out. I grew up in an environment in which respect for others, regardless of their job or income, was a given. But soon after I climbed the corporate ladder, I learned that the mutual respect practiced by the working class exceeded that of most of the business elite. If I had to select the one attribute that I believe separated me from many other CEOs, it was my respect for the individual. I can't even count the number of times when I witnessed a fellow CEO rudely snap at a flight attendant or waiter for no apparent reason, flaunting his functional, hierarchical position as if to suggest that he was king and the support person was a serf. I refuse to tolerate that treatment of fellow human beings regardless of their lot in life and I do my best to go exactly the opposite way. I'm not alone in this. There are those exceptional leaders who have maintained their sense of humanity despite their power and money. One such individual is Ken Langone, one of the founders of Home Depot. I once called him for career advice. He met with me that very afternoon, and unbeknownst to me, he flew from Atlanta to New York just for the meeting. You can't put a price on that kind of humanity and friendship.

When I was CEO of PaineWebber, and still today, I take the time to talk to the security guard when I come into work. I had an ongoing dialogue with the elevator operator in my old PaineWebber building, encouraging him to stick with his night schooling as he strove to better his life. I still go out of my way during the holidays to give something extra, separate from a tip, to everyone who works at my favorite restaurants, from the dishwasher to the maître d'. When I bring business associates to lunch or dinner, they still comment on how I seem to be treated so well. Waiters who are not even serving our table come over to say hello. I shake each of their hands when they stop by. This is such a simple act, yet it is rarely done. When was the last time you walked into a restaurant and shook the hand of the bartender or any waiter or waitress you encounter? That simple gesture costs you nothing, but it earns you incalculable respect.

To this day, when a fellow CEO mistreats a person for no reason in front of me, I wait for the embarrassed person to move out of hearing range, and then I inform the CEO that he or she cannot treat people that way in my presence. It is interesting that usually they become apologetic and immediately change their demeanor toward the individual they previously belittled. I do not suggest that you practice such candor with your superiors. Instead, try to be a role model. You will find that if you treat people with respect, so will your employees. It has always been well known throughout every organization I have ever led that you can't work for me if you mistreat people.

Treating individuals with respect isn't just a question of morality and an activity for outside the workplace. It yields quantifiable financial advantages inside the office. Remember that the plane doesn't get up without the ground crew.

I once worked for a chairman who would call a trader who, let's say, lost $1 million on a proprietary trade (one in which the firm itself is looking to profit from the transaction rather than relying on commissions from the trade). He would beat the living hell out of the trader and suggest that he or she was putting the firm out of business. I can assure you the only motivational button that chairman was pushing was the self-destruct button. The trader would subsequently be too risk averse to trade; would lose self-esteem, which resulted in isolation from his or her peer group; and would eventually disparage the firm, internally as well as externally. All traders occasionally have losing trades. When I took over control of the trading desks in that firm, I politely told the browbeating chairman he was not to call the traders directly but was instead to call me. I never called a trader to complain about a loss; I called only to congratulate him or her on a gain. If the chairman saw a losing day and asked, "Who did it?" I would respond by saying, "I did." "No, no," he would insist. "Who made the trade?" Again I would reply, "I did it. My division. My watch. My loss."

Treating traders with respect as human beings and shielding them in downtimes from the attacks of the chairman resulted in a culture that led to better results. Instead of fearfully waiting for accusatory calls from the chairman, the traders would occasionally call me and say remorsefully, "Joe, I let you down today; I lost $1 million on my position." I would ask what happened. If the trader said the loss was due to a prediction for the market that didn't come through, I'd ask if the trader still felt confident of the prediction. If the trader continued to have confidence, and I agreed with his or her view, I would instruct him or her to then double up the position. That approach told the traders that I understood their business and that I retained the utmost confidence in them. As a result, I was able to build up the trader's self-esteem in a crisis moment rather than tearing it down. That trader would become an advocate of the firm, both internally and externally, and our trading profits soared.

Respecting subordinates as human beings was more than just a morale-boosting device; it yielded priceless intelligence. I've come to believe that half of good management is asking good questions. Whether I was assessing risk versus reward or deciding how best to deploy assets, my willingness to ask good commonsense questions of those on the front line provided me with the intelligence and information vital to making effective decisions. When the captain doesn't know who's in the engine room or what's going on down there, the ship is in trouble.

During my years at PaineWebber, my lieutenants often marveled at the amount of time I would spend listening to what they would characterize as drivel. They would ask me why I wasted so much time on someone. I always answered that if time permitted, it was the act of giving someone a chance to offer an opinion, however ill judged or foolish that opinion, that enabled me to gather intelligence about the firm. Even if the idea was without any value as information, allowing the individual to voice it gave me the opportunity to subsequently lead him or her in the opposite direction without dissent. I explained to my lieutenants that if I didn't listen, then that individual—if not the entire organization—would never believe that I respected someone else's point of view. Employees needed to know that I respected their opinion no matter their position or how off-center their idea might have seemed to me. My job as an executive was to listen, gently massage their opinion to one that supported where I wanted to go, and have the employee leave my office feeling that he or she had made a positive contribution. Furthermore, no one, including me, has the patent on being right. There were times when my employees had a better idea or a better way of doing things than I did.

Of course, there were times, particularly in moments of crisis, when I couldn't afford to spend the amount of time it takes to show this respect for everyone's ideas by giving them a chance to express them. That's why I exercised what I call the

95-5 rule. Ninety-five percent of the time I encouraged all my employees to express their point of view, even if it was contrary to my own. However, when I said, "We're in the 5 percent," I meant there was no time for debate: they had to do what I told them to do. My direct reports eventually were able to figure things out just by reading my body language. They would say, "Joe, we know, we're in the five," and abandon the debate and follow direction.

Sometimes you need to exercise the 5 percent rule in support of your intuition or gut rather than in response to a crisis. In early 1998, I called in my head of capital markets, Steve Baum, an excellent manager. I informed him that I wanted him to sell out our proprietary position in Russian sovereign debt. I always made it a priority to know our inventory on every desk around the world because those positions constituted some of the greatest risks or exposures to the firm. Steve proceeded to reassure me that no sovereign had ever defaulted on its debt, and he estimated that our firm was going to profit approximately $7.5 million from the position. I responded that I just didn't feel right about that inventory position, and I wanted us out. After a lively debate, I reminded Steven that this "is not a democracy. You're in the five. Now sell us out."

Three months later, Russia defaulted. There was blood all over the Street as most, if not all, emerging market debt positions precipitously dropped in value. (Emerging markets are those nations that are moving toward becoming advanced markets. They are generally developed sufficiently enough to have a financial infrastructure, but not enough to have in place a great deal of market regulation. Because of their inherent risk, they offer the potential for high returns. Emerging market debt is an asset class that includes bonds, loans, and other credit obligations issued by governments or corporations within emerging market nations.) PaineWebber was the only firm I know of that finished the year with no losses in sovereign or emerging market debt.

Steve approached me at our employee Christmas party the following December and asked, "Joe, how the hell did you know Russia was going to default?" I answered, "I didn't. But as I was watching President Yeltsin at the time on TV, he appeared sickly and I didn't want us to be invested in a country where the leader might be courting with heaven's door."

I winked and added, "Sometimes it's better to be lucky than good."

Showing respect for your subordinates' humanity isn't just a matter of chatting with them or letting them express their ideas. There are managerial practices and policies you can enact that will help institutionalize respect for humanity in your organization.

At PaineWebber, we began with an understanding that each employee deserved to know the company's expectations of the tasks they were assigned and how well they did in fulfilling those tasks. By memorializing the responsibilities and authorities of every position in the hierarchy, we documented that the individual holding that position was due respect for the job he or she did. In addition, by providing agreed-on performance expectations and goals, we created an environment in which human beings could be shown respect for transcending their places in the hierarchy.

Each position within our organization, including my own, had a job charter that described the duties of the position and, whenever possible, the level of authority that the position carried—for example: "The receptionist will screen all calls, direct them to the appropriate manager, and, if necessary, will record a message for the manager. He or she will greet and appropriately direct all guests who come to our offices. The receptionist has the responsibility and authority to schedule utilization of the conference rooms."

By delineating the responsibilities of the receptionist position within the job charter, we responded to an appropriate employee concern: "What does my boss want me to do?" By articulating the responsibility of booking the conference rooms and simultaneously giving him or her the authority to schedule, we empowered the receptionist to succeed with that task.

Every job charter included measurement standards as to how performance of the job would be evaluated. Certain positions, particularly managerial, had changing goals each year. Those positions required a goal-setting discussion with the individual's immediate supervisor. For example, in a given year, a manager of a branch office at PaineWebber may have had a revenue increase goal of more than 10 percent, a profit improvement goal of 12 percent, and a market share improvement goal of 2 percent. Depending on the performance the year before, or perhaps from a material change in the forecast business environment, those percentages might change dramatically from year to year.

Performance was judged by no more than five critical objectives, and those objectives didn't have the same weight for each employee. Two of the criteria were revenue generation and cost reduction. A manager who had an excellent track record as a revenue producer would receive a higher weighting for cost reduction. We wanted our compensation to recognize strengths, but it was more important to use compensation to drive improvement of weaknesses. It was essential that an individual had an opportunity to discuss, and to some degree negotiate, those goals and objectives with his or her immediate superior. This fostered ownership of the goals rather than a view of them as a sterile mandate.

Most good corporations have a performance review process in place, but many do not have a formalized development review process. This was another of our innovations at PaineWebber. It provided an opportunity for a supervisor to get a better understanding of the employee's aspirations and highlight strengths and weaknesses to the employee. Having developmental reviews was also a way we could demonstrate that we saw every individual in our firm, regardless of his or her position in the hierarchy, as someone who had the potential to grow and increase his or her contribution.

The developmental review was conducted midyear between an employee and his or her immediate supervisor, and it was clearly postured as developmental rather than performance related. The employee was encouraged to submit, in writing, topics that he or she wanted to discuss. The primary objectives of the developmental review were for the supervisor to assist the employee in mapping out a career path, discuss a plan of action—such as training courses—to assist the employee in the attainment of his or her career goals, and foster a better relationship between the supervisor and the employee through better understanding of each other's goals and priorities. The supervisor sent the employee a written review within thirty days subsequent to the meeting that included a remedial plan if necessary.

Conducting these additional reviews was time-consuming, but it helped create a culture of mutual respect and fostered a commonality of purpose. I believe it had a positive return on investment.

At PaineWebber, we also made sure our compensation policies rewarded merit and didn't just automatically give increases to individuals because of their positions. We predicated the size of the merit increase pool by the firm's profitability, coupled, in some cases, with an inflation index. If our total salary base was, for example, $20 million, and we settled on a merit increase of 3 percent, then we would have a pool of $600,000. Too many managers automatically give each of their employees the 3 percent increase. What we did was give a good performer 6 percent and a poor performer nothing. This approach forced an evaluation of performance and created a meritocracy, in contrast to the typical method that resonates of socialism and rewards mediocrity.

The amount of the bonus an employee earned was based on an approach similar to that used in awarding increases. For example, a department manager's total compensation package might be $75,000 in salary, a stock award equal to $10,000 worth of stock valued on December 31, and a bonus range of between $10,000 and $25,000. A manager whose performance was judged to have "met requirements" qualified for a bonus at the low end of the range. If performance was judged to have "exceeded requirements," the manager qualified for a bonus in the middle of the range. Only if the manager's performance rating was "far exceeded requirements" did he or she qualify for a bonus at the top end of the range. By creating sliding scales for both merit increases and bonuses, we demonstrated to employees that we valued their individual efforts more than the title they held.

I deployed several types of interpersonal exchanges at PaineWebber to demonstrate my respect for employees' humanity. Some critics categorized these intangibles as manipulative and unnecessary. Admittedly, there were times I hyped an event or an issue to get my constituents to "drink the Kool-Aid." But the intent was pure and the result equated to a better situation for the firm's partners—who include the employees themselves. So why not?

As in most other sales organizations, the top salespeople at PaineWebber were also given additional recognition for their stellar performance. I always targeted the top 20 percent of the sales force, which totaled fourteen hundred people: 20 percent of seven thousand financial advisors. Those fourteen hundred people were divided into three groups:

- The Chairman's Club consisted of two hundred financial advisors producing $2 million or more in revenues.
- The President's Club was made up of four hundred financial advisors producing between $1 million and $1.999 million in revenues.
- The Pacesetters Club contained eight hundred financial advisors who produced between $500,000 and $999,999 in revenues.

The specific financial qualifications for the three groups were reset each year based on market conditions and projections. I raised the bar almost every year, and they always came through.

The Chairman's Club was rewarded with a four-day trip at a destination resort or a foreign city. The President's Club was sent on a three-day trip to a domestic destination resort, like the Phoenician in Arizona. The members of the Pacesetters Club were divided regionally and sent on two-day celebrations in their areas. Spouses of the financial advisors were invited as well.

Senior management and their spouses attended each trip. Each day of the event had scheduled business meetings during the mornings and leisure events, such as golf and tennis, in the afternoons. We also scheduled a voluntary spouse-only meeting where I met with the spouses, giving them an overview of the firm and our strategy. I always held a lengthy question-and-answer session with them, stressing my gratitude for their support and for that of their significant others. Each evening there was a dinner with entertainment. When they returned to their rooms each evening, the financial advisors and spouses found "pillow gifts" as well as a formal thank-you message from the firm's management. The last night's celebration included named entertainment. For example, one Chairman's Club event featured a performance by Frankie Valli and another the Pointer Sisters. On the final evening of these events, I personally walked to each table and thanked the financial advisors and their spouses for their support and wished them and their families a healthy, prosperous year.

In our current economic environment, many in Congress and in the media are attacking these types of incentive trips. Certainly they should be curtailed, if not eliminated, when a firm is not doing well or if a firm seeks taxpayer money to survive. In good times, however, they more than pay for themselves. They allow the CEO to amalgamate in one place the firm's decentralized sales leaders to gain their support for his or her strategy, win the support of their spouses, and, by moving the productivity bar up each year as a prerequisite to attend, improve profitability for shareholders.

I didn't limit intangibles to the firm's high achievers. As chairman and CEO, I spoke to every training school class. I gave a one-hour presentation on how to succeed in the business, and then held a thirty-minute open question-and-answer session. Prior to the presentation, I introduced myself to each of the three hundred trainee participants with a handshake and a personal word.

I believe that walking to some fifty tables at recognition dinners and acknowledging my appreciation for my employees' efforts, and personally shaking the hands of each class of trainees, helped set the tone that at PaineWebber, we respected everyone, whatever their status in the organization. To this day, I still receive letters from those who attended trainee sessions that state they never forgot that their chairman took the time to acknowledge them as individuals.

Most human resource experts suggest that managers should stay away from nonwork-related problems that their employees may have. I reject that notion. If you're going to respect your employees' humanity, you need to recognize that people's work lives affect their personal lives, and their personal lives affect their work lives. If an employee's personal problem affected his or her performance, then indirectly I, as a manager, had a problem too. I encouraged my managers to be open to assisting employees with their personal problems. I didn't want my managers inserting themselves in the middle of divorce proceedings, but I told them that it was important to let employees know it was okay to vent or ask for advice or help.

One afternoon while president of PaineWebber, I received a troubling phone call. A young manager called with the upsetting news that his fifteen-month-old son had been diagnosed with cancer in both of his eyes. Ultimately I told him to find the best specialist in the world, and I didn't care if that specialist was in Switzerland. I told him he was to take as much time off as his family needed and to send me the bill for his son's medical care. While he did have to take some time off, he was able to find the care his son needed here in the United States. This young manager eventually became president of a major division within the firm. His son, who is legally blind, is enjoying a fulfilling life in college today. And the manager never did send me the bill.

This involvement with the personal lives of employees wasn't limited to my senior management team. One Christmas week I was manning the telephones in the executive offices. I made it a practice to give my direct reports and support staff every Christmas Eve off so they could spend the time at home with their family. A call came in from a former employee, a sales assistant who had been laid off earlier in the month. The woman was sobbing at a laundromat in New Hampshire: her severance check hadn't arrived, and as a result, she couldn't afford to buy Christmas presents for her children. I told her to look in the telephone book, find the nearest Western Union office, give me the address, and I would personally wire her the money she was due. I told her that when the severance check from the company arrived, she could pay me back. She found the address, and I wired the money from my personal account.

It was the right thing to do regardless of whether it had a positive impact on the firm.

When, after Christmas, I told this story to one of my lieutenants, he expressed doubt that the woman would ever repay the money I had sent her. After all, she had been laid off by the firm. When her personal check repaying my loan arrived a few weeks later, I showed it to him. The event had a major impact on his attitude. Months later, there was a story on the evening news about a young paralyzed boy whose wheelchair had been stolen, and I watched him respond to it by sending a check to pay for a replacement wheelchair. My reflexive treatment of a former employee as a valuable human being deserving of help erased some cynicism in the heart of another executive. That resulted in his becoming an even more valuable contributor to the firm's culture and bottom line, and more important, in leading an already charitable person to become even more philanthropic.

I believe in the personal touch. Each year at Christmas, I personally select a unique gift for each of my direct reports and their spouses. I spend months in advance thinking of a creative gift, and I try to do something for them that they wouldn't or couldn't do for themselves. For example, one year the men on my gift list received a custom-made walnut case with a brass plate inscribed with the message, "To [named individual] and his fellow big hitters." Inside the box were nine baseballs with authenticated signatures from players like Mickey Mantle, Ted Williams, Willie Mays, and Nolan Ryan. For the millennium, I presented the women on my gift list with gold necklaces that were designed around two-thousand-year-old gold coins issued by the Emperor Augustus Caesar. I personally select and pay for each of these gifts. Along with each gift I handwrite a special letter not just to my subordinate but to his or her spouse as well. Writing those letters typically takes about three days of concentrated time, but it is worth every moment.

Although I can't tangibly measure the ultimate impact of these gifts, I do believe they have contributed to the tenure of my direct reports. The executives who reported directly to me did so for an average of thirteen years each, and that continuity of management greatly contributed to our success.

I am not suggesting that you need to be so extravagant in your gift selection in order to demonstrate your regard for your direct reports as human beings. I *am* suggesting that you never delegate the selection or purchase of these gifts to a third party, such as your administrative assistant. What is more important is the time that you personally extend on your subordinates' behalf.

The connectivity you establish with the personal touch is attained by more than writing letters and showing appreciation through gift giving. It is gained primarily by expressing your care for your constituents as individuals. Those constituents include your clients. In 1993 that philosophy was severely tested. At the time, I was serving as president of PaineWebber Consumer Markets. While I was attending a recognition trip for some of our best financial advisors in Phoenix, I received a call from our chairman, who asked me to return to New York and evaluate a dire situation that had evolved within the company's asset management division.

The asset management division had created a short-term government-security-weighted mutual fund that was postured to provide safety and a higher yield than what was available then within money market funds. It was a highly successful offering, accumulating close to $1 billion of our clients' money. Unfortunately, the fund underperformed almost immediately and began to lose some of its net asset value. The management team within the asset management company was perplexed and reacted by retreating into a cave. That served only to exacerbate the situation not only with very angry clients but with my very angry brokers who had recommended the fund to their clients in the first place.

When I hurried back from Phoenix, I quickly discovered that the fund was peppered with several high-octane derivatives to enhance its yield. (High-octane derivatives are high-risk, high-reward securities whose price is based on underlying "assets" that could be anything from stocks to average rainfall.) The original prospectus allowed the use of these types of speculative securities; however, it also stated that they would be used sparingly, if at all. In fact, the selling materials used two months earlier stated that there was no current intent to engage in that type of investment strategy.

I formed a due diligence team made up of fixed-income specialists, traders, legal counsel, and mutual fund accountants. I had them create a hypothetical fund that mirrored the original fund except the hypothetical fund would not have any of the derivative positions that had resulted in a loss within the original fund. Any derivative position in the original fund that had produced a profit was allowed to remain. The difference in value between the hypothetical fund without the losing high-octane securities and the current live fund was $37 million.

Two days after returning to New York, I told our chairman that we should write a check for $37 million, deposit the money in the fund, and remove the toxic nonperforming securities. The markets had moved against all types of fixed-income securities, and investors were facing a loss in the fund regardless of the losses incurred by the derivative positions. However, in our fund's case, they were losing an additional $37 million.

My chairman suggested that I was nuts. Our general counsel concurred, noting that we had the legal right to use those high-octane securities. My response was that we would ultimately lose a technical argument based on our stated "intent," and furthermore, if we didn't take a lead in rectifying the situation, we would face serious disintermediation of the remaining funds being managed within the asset management company. We were already facing growing unrest among our financial advisors, who had been placed in a precarious position: they were forced to side with their clients in admonishing the firm for the perceived violations within the fund.

I ultimately won the day and PaineWebber wrote a check for $37 million and deposited it into the fund. To this day, the chairman will still argue with me that we shouldn't have written that check. However, I think my instincts were proven right. Our asset management company went on to grow by multiple billions of dollars of assets. Our financial advisors became advocates of our firm and our values. Finally, subsequent rulings by our regulators often noted that PaineWebber stood up and did the right thing for clients without being forced or asked to. The value of the goodwill created with multiple constituencies was considerable. In my mind, all of this was worth the $37 million. Yes, it was a lot of money. But I would rather feel the pain and deal with the emotion than cower and hide. That will cost you your self-respect, your confidence, and your ability to lead others, all of which are priceless. As a saying goes, if you're going down in a ball of flames, you might as well light your own match.

As I'd hoped, the respect management showed for the humanity of employees eventually started changing the Wild West culture we'd inherited at PaineWebber, and it had an impact on the attitudes and actions of everyone in the organization. I saw the evidence in 1998, when Russia defaulted on its sovereign debt obligations and emerging market debt worldwide got caught up in the contagion. Wall Street experienced immense pain as emerging market debt positions had to be marked down precipitously. Earnings were decimated, and a litany of layoffs ensued. At PaineWebber we were contemplating a significant downsizing of approximately seven hundred people. Our employee base was very apprehensive, as were employees throughout Wall Street.

In response, I made an executive decision that shocked my management team: I held a nationwide conference call in which I announced that there would be no merit increases that year and that management bonuses would be reduced. I explained that this sacrifice by some would enable the firm to keep seven hundred of their fellow employees working. I didn't rule out a possible future layoff if conditions continued to deteriorate; however, I wanted that reaction to be our last resort.

This is a tactic that can be used only rarely and in times of real crisis. Would it work in today's current economic crisis? I'm not privy to proprietary details on the financial condition of the larger firms in the financial services industry, so I do not know whether such a move would provide sufficient relief given the unprecedented economic conditions. I do know that the only thing worse for employee morale than widespread lay-offs is going out of business.

In 1998 when I made the decision to spread the pain at PaineWebber, I was somewhat apprehensive about the response my decision would elicit. I was, after all, telling thousands of individuals who had been expecting to be rewarded for their hard work and excellent results that they would not be receiving the increases they had in fact earned.

But instead of hearing from my managers about staff grumbling or anger, I received over a thousand e-mails, letters, and telephone calls from individual employees offering thanks, many noting that "this is why I love this firm." It was during this crisis that I knew a culture of respecting individuals for their shared humanity had become part of the DNA of PaineWebber.

Ironically, it wasn't long after this realization that I faced a looming threat to this wonderful culture that we'd worked so hard for so long to create. The evolving nature of communications and geopolitical interdependencies requires that many institutions globalize in order to survive, and that is certainly the case for the financial services industry. When I was president of PaineWebber, I concluded that achieving that goal required more than just the desire: it required the capability of becoming a global power brand. To achieve that would require extensive capital footings, an untraditional trait for Americans called patience, and a willingness to adjust to disparate cultures.

There is no doubt that the democratization of the formerly communist Eastern European nations, the entrepreneurialism of the Pacific Rim, and the stabilization of Latin

America constitute immense opportunities for American know-how and capital. But the way you participate and at what risk to your franchise are issues.

At PaineWebber we decided to view the world through the metaphor of a geographical target of three concentric circles. In the center—the bull's-eye—was the United States. The next ring was industrialized Europe, anchored by the United Kingdom, France, and Germany. The outer ring consisted of the Pacific Rim nations. We concluded that going global on our own would be a mistake for PaineWebber.

Our assessment of the industrialized world, in the context of the financial services industry, was that there was not one country in Europe that did not already have a bulge bracket player such as ourselves. What would make us think that the Ugly American could land on the shores of, say, Germany, and beat Deutsche Bank? Could we really be a franchise player? Did we have the capital, the patience, and the willingness to adjust to other cultures?

The reverse was equally true. Deutsche Bank hadn't been successful in cracking the U.S. market. Nomura failed in its efforts to sell U.S. securities to U.S. institutions. Financial services firms had succeeded only within their geographical arena, or in sales in which they had a competitive advantage. Nomura succeeded in Japan and in selling Japanese securities to U.S. institutions. Deutsche Bank managed money successfully in its Germany fund for U.S. investors. We believed that we at PaineWebber could be a major provider of U.S. securities to foreign institutions, but we doubted we could alone build a competitive franchise in another country that already had a dominant local player.

We decided to go where no financial services firm had gone before. We opted for a strategy that would maximize our national franchise, maintain our unique culture, and allow us to strategically ally with a foreign bulge bracket player within the European and Pacific Rim circles of our global target—a player that could provide our U.S. clients with superior products when needed. This firm would in turn represent our products to their clients when they needed access to U.S. products. The result was the merger of UBS and PaineWebber.

The initial inquiry came from UBS. They sent their president of the group executive board, Luqman Arnold, to meet with us. He suggested at a luncheon that they were perhaps interested in a strategic alliance. I became quickly convinced that this meeting was much more than a "let's get to know you" facade, as their knowledge of our firm exemplified more than curiosity. Several months later, they returned with a proposition that our two firms merge, with UBS as the parent. Don Marron, our chairman, and I, as president, entered into intense negotiations. Don secured a record price for our shareholders. John Costas of UBS and I were given the responsibility to integrate the two firms.

John and I decided that we would make all integration decisions, and our decisions would be final. Any new construct would have three years to prove or right itself. At the end of the third year, we would entertain a change if convinced it was for the better. This approach removed all of the infighting that naturally occurs when merging firms' captains are fighting for their own turf. The three-year moratorium allowed ample time for merged departments or divisions to work out their differences, and precluded anyone trying to retrade the decision.

This approach worked brilliantly, and the UBS PaineWebber merger went down as one of the most successful in Wall Street history.

In recent years, things have not gone as well for the firm. Since my departure at the end of 2004, UBS has taken a series of monumental missteps, most of which originated in Switzerland. The accusations relative to moving U.S. clients to locations or into products to avoid taxation were not against U.S. financial advisors. These controversial tax strategies emanated from private bankers sent to the United States from the private bank domiciled in Switzerland. Whether true or false, such accusations created negative perceptions and brand destruction. Coupled with the immense write-downs (losses) associated with mortgage-backed securities, derivatives, and credit default swaps, the destruction of goodwill has been incalculable. Given the Swiss reputation for confidentiality and superb risk management, it's hard to see how they could have gotten themselves into this precarious position.

My observations, while serving on the Group Executive Board in Switzerland, have led me to believe that this situation did not arise because of some premeditated, nefarious conduct. Rather it came from a culture that relies too much on process and too little on management. At the Swiss headquarters, every door was closed. Meetings between peers had to be scheduled. The board meetings followed a strict protocol of going page by page through a board book developed by staff. There was no strategic dialogue and very few challenges. No hallway chitchat took place, and there was no opportunity for body language interpretations. It was run just by the book, just by the process. I got a sense that the staff, the process, the book, was running the firm. In my opinion, a process culture may work within an insular homogeneous enterprise or when constructing a watch. It does not work within a global enterprise that requires cross-border cooperation, understanding, and, above all, transparency.

In many ways, the challenges facing UBS are a reflection of those facing Switzerland. The legacy value proposition of confidentiality, of providing a safe haven for black or illegitimate deposits, and for tax avoidance, are gone or going. Other European nations will not tolerate losing capital to Switzerland, and some have already begun to respond with amnesty for repatriated assets. The United States will not tolerate tax schemes that violate fair assessment of its citizens, and global intellectual talent will not take direction solely from an operations manual.

Of course, at the time of the merger, I didn't anticipate the development of any of these problems. I saw only clear sailing ahead for UBS PaineWebber. But as I soon learned, terrible events can emerge from the brightest and sunniest of skies.

"Joe's whole career is commitment to his country, from serving in the Special Forces to his support for the police. Joe's efforts as part of the steering committee to get Wall Street back [after September 11], to get the stock exchange back in what was really a miraculously short period of time meant a great deal to the economy, to the national economy, to the economy of the city. Maybe the most important contribution was to give us a boost in morale just when we needed it. And the idea that the stock exchange could come back by that Monday after September 11 and actually function gave us a kind of sense that we could rebuild, that we could come back, and that we could stand up against what had been done to us."

—RUDOLPH GIULIANI

Chapter Eight

SEPTEMBER 11, 2001

There are times when the complexity and uniqueness of the events of our lives, which so often seem random and unconnected, fall into place. Then suddenly, in a dramatic moment of tragedy or triumph—and sometimes both—things become clear; the pieces all fit together. On September 11, 2001, and in the weeks following, I found myself in a situation that demanded drawing on all the skills and experience I'd acquired in my life and previous careers.

Our country faced a horrific truth on that day. For the first time since Pearl Harbor, we were attacked on our own shores by a sinister enemy. The vivid recollection of watching two jet airliners crash into the World Trade Center towers, causing thousands of deaths, will remain imprinted in our consciousness forever. As the second plane crashed into the second tower, millions of Americans witnessed it live, on camera. Seeing friends, neighbors, associates, and employees jumping from the towers to escape the flames, and falling to their deaths, and the subsequent collapse of the buildings, tested our ability to reason. Was this actually happening? Could our great nation be this vulnerable to attack? As the day proceeded and the reports of a plane crashing into the Pentagon, killing hundreds more Americans, and of the heroic efforts of the passengers causing a fourth plane to crash in the fields of Pennsylvania, our worst fears were validated. Yes it was happening, and yes, we as a free society, are that vulnerable.

No one knows for sure exactly what criteria the terrorists used in selecting their targets. However, there is no doubt that the Pentagon, the New York financial district, and the White House, which was the possible target of the plane that crashed in Pennsylvania, were selected at least in part because they are icons that exemplify the worldwide position of America relative to our military, financial, and political might. The terrorists achieved their initial goal of shocking our nation, as well as the rest of the world, by attacking the largest symbol of democracy and capitalism on its own shores. I do not believe, however, that they counted on the strength and resolve that America displayed subsequent to the attacks. All Americans rallied to support those who were harmed as well as their families. People from all corners of our nation traveled to the target sites to physically, morally, and financially support the victims and the brave firefighters, police officers, and emergency responders who were in harm's way. I must admit the sadness and anger I felt were somewhat countered by the immense pride I experienced from watching us come together as one nation to deal with this tragedy.

I learned of the attacks on the World Trade Center while having breakfast in my room at my favorite New York City hotel. I was about to turn off CNBC and walk across the street to the UBS offices when I saw a report about the first plane hitting. The damage looked too big to have come from a small private plane. Just then the second plane hit the other tower, and I knew we were under attack.

I rushed to the office and got the management team together on the telephone. Since we were located in midtown, the immediate effect wasn't nearly as traumatic as that experienced by firms headquartered downtown. Still, I needed to gather facts. I asked for a head count of any employees we might have located in or near the towers, and I learned we had five people missing downtown. (Two were outside the towers when jet fuel fell on them, leaving them badly burned. Three others were inside the buildings when they were struck.) My thoughts next turned to the staff at our Weehawken facility, located directly across the Hudson River from the World Trade Center. We all had lost friends, but they had a close-up view of people jumping to their deaths and the towers collapsing.

In my role as the leader of UBS PaineWebber I faced three immediate concerns: my employee, my clients, and business continuity.

My employees were in shock over the attack; they were fearful of what could happen next, worried about the condition of their five fellow employees, and grieving the multiple friends, associates, and neighbors who lost their lives. Many of their spouses and children did not make a distinction between Weehawken, New Jersey; midtown Manhattan; and Wall Street. To their families, we all worked "on" Wall Street, and Wall Street was certainly a target.

My clients had entrusted their assets to us. They were fearful about the safety of those assets, unsure whether our firm and the rest of Wall Street would be able to reopen, and worried about further attacks.

Fortunately for PaineWebber, we had established both disaster recovery and business continuity plans. (These are not to be confused with contingency plans, which are designed to react to short falls in the firm's anticipated results.) My entire executive committee was involved in the preparation of these plans. Little did we know that we would ever have to initiate them, and little did we know how effective they would be, because no simulation or training exercise can equal events never before experienced.

Our plans worked exceedingly well, with the exception of being weak in one area: directing fleeing employees. Every fire drill conducted at every firm always assumes that employees reenter the building. For many of our competitors, there were no buildings left to reenter after the attack. The employees of these downtown firms were directionless, and we learned from their mistakes and the corresponding shortfall in our plans. We subsequently made appropriate adjustments.

It was imperative that I take a high profile as the chief executive. During crises, people want to be led. They want clear, concise instruction and crave a sense that everything will be fine. This was a time when I told my staff we were in "the five," a time when I wasn't open to listening to others' opinions or ideas. I immediately focused on our organization's problems and started to develop solutions.

To deal with the shock and fear, on September 12 I moved immediately to form and address a series of "town meetings" of no more than two hundred people each, out of the approximately three thousand people we had working in

Manhattan and Weehawken. I supplemented those meetings with a national telephone conference call every morning and afternoon for more than a week, addressing all employees. Sadly, our three employees never made it out of the towers. The two who were just outside the buildings ultimately lost their lives, after remaining in critical condition for two weeks. We kept all of our employees updated as to their conditions and provided moral and financial support for their families.

During the town meetings, I emphasized that within the Muslim world, as well as within any other group, there are minority factions that defer to violence or, in extreme cases, even genocide. I insisted that I would not tolerate any form of bigotry or blame of innocent people. Period. Senior executives often underestimate their employees. When you give the general population the facts and show that you share their humanity and sensitivities, they always do the right thing.

I urged my employees with young children to realize that even if their children were putting up a brave front, they were worried that their mom or dad was in harm's way. I encouraged the employees to explain the difference between midtown Manhattan, Weehawken, and Wall Street to their children. I prompted them to open up and vent their experience to their children and to induce their children to do the same. And finally, I told them to, if necessary, take some time off to spend with their children to deal with their anxiety. With my pressing issues at UBS PaineWebber addressed, I next had to prepare for what would become a historic meeting to discuss the reopening of the New York Stock Exchange.

In a crisis, truth, facts, and problems must be dealt with without regard to expediency, postmortems, politics, and even, at times, patriotism. These tenets were seriously tested immediately following 9/11. The New York Stock Exchange is located a stone's throw from what had been the World Trade Center towers. So were the headquarters locations of large financial institutions, such as Merrill Lynch, Goldman Sachs, and Lehman Brothers. All of the major financial institutions in the downtown area of New York City were forced to abandon their buildings. Several of their buildings would never be occupied again due to the structural damage caused by the collapse of the two towers.

As Wall Street is the epicenter of the worldwide capital market, the subsequent evacuation of the target area stopped the financial markets in their tracks. Most of the communications lines linking the money center banks, brokerage firms, and exchanges were out. The transmission switching centers were under water. Federal fund wire transfers were inaccessible. The interdependencies that all financial firms had with the communication centers domiciled in and around Wall Street became painfully apparent. One major bank, for instance, processed more than 70 percent of all wire transfers for the entire community. Its system was down and its backup "hot site" was not functioning. Fortunately, in that case, the New York Federal Reserve Bank interceded and provided assurances that all wire transfers would be guaranteed. It was imperative to get our capital market up and functioning again. While the search for bodies was still going on, thousands of system technicians, engineers, phone service installers, and electricians descended on Wall Street to try to get the financial system back up and running.

On September 12, top executives representing Wall Street, banking, energy, and communications, met in a large conference room at Bear Stearns' headquarters in midtown Manhattan. Representing the federal government were Harvey Pitt, chairman of the Securities and Exchange Commission, and undersecretary of the Treasury, Peter Fisher. Among the Wall Street executives present, besides me, were Richard Grasso, CEO of the New York Stock Exchange; James Cayne, CEO of Bear Stearns; Phil Purcell, CEO of Morgan Stanley; Steve Hammerman, vice chairman of Merrill Lynch; John Mack, co-CEO of Credit Suisse First Boston; Richard Fuld, CEO of Lehman Brothers; and Sandy Weill, CEO and chairman of Citigroup. Also present were Lawrence Babbio, vice chairman of Verizon, and Kevin Burke, president and chief operating officer of ConEdison.

Secretary Fisher was there to encourage the group to reopen the New York Stock Exchange the next day: Thursday, September 13. His impassioned plea was centered around the importance of not letting the attacks disrupt the world capital markets. His message was that we could not let these terrorists achieve another one of their major objectives: financial havoc throughout the world. As you can imagine, an immense patriotic rally ensued throughout the room. It was wonderful to witness and experience such camaraderie and collaboration between such competitive "gods" and "heads of state." My enthusiasm quickly abated, however, as I sensed that as a group, we were not dealing with the facts or with a truthful assessment of the situation. I had a foreboding, a feeling that we were courting a potential disaster.

In the midst of the rambunctious discussion echoing around the room I pounded my fist on the conference table in front of me and yelled out words to the effect of "just a minute" or "time out." The room went silent. My reputation as a can-do executive, veteran, and patriot thankfully gave me the credibility to put forth a complete opposite point of view. Although they might disagree with me, there was no way they could question my motivation or my patriotism. I proceeded to outline the realities of our situation. I pointed out that of all the firms represented at the table, my firm, UBS PaineWebber, was least physically affected by the attack because our headquarters was located in midtown and our marketing, operations, and systems facilities were located out of harm's way in Weehawken, New Jersey. Yet I believed even we couldn't be ready to open the next day.

I reminded several of the firms that their management teams and New York employees were scattered around multiple locations, their communication lines were no longer operable, temporary cables routing their orders to the floor of the New York Stock Exchange were literally hanging out of windows, and the communication switching centers were still underwater. Of the Wall Street leaders gathered in that room, I was one of the few who had experience on the operational end of the business; I knew what went on in the trenches. I prophesied that if we attempted to reopen our markets the next day, our enthusiasm would be rewarded by a functional crash of our operating system. A premature reopening would result in a failure that could shatter confidence in the worldwide capital market. I suggested that we would be playing right into the hands of the terrorists by giving them what they wanted in the first place: financial havoc. I passionately argued that the truth is never wrong: at the cost of staying closed another two days, we could use the weekend to test our recovery initiatives to ensure that we could sustain a market opening.

An argument ensued. I was pretty much alone in my position and got into a somewhat heated discussion with Peter Fisher. I suggested that we could trade and process orders within the dealer markets that served over-the-counter and certain fixed-income securities, but there was no way that the system could accommodate the auction market that traded listed stocks and bonds. At one point, I insisted to him and others that in this crisis, we had to consider the unintended consequences of our actions. I warned that "when you push down on the waterbed, you had better understand where it is going to pop up." We had to fully think through what could happen.

I knew I was beginning to make sense to several of my peers as their initial exuberant reactions began to move toward pragmatic reasoning. I finally turned to Steve Hammerman of Merrill Lynch and said: "Please don't give me any of your bullish-on-America crap right now. Look me in the eye, and tell me your firm can be ready to open on Thursday." Steve excused himself from the table and left the room. He came back ten minutes later and stated that there was no way they could be ready. The honesty of Merrill Lynch, the largest brokerage firm in the world, saved the day. Immediately following Merrill Lynch's assessment, John Mack stepped up and said, "I agree with Joe." At that point, Richard Grasso announced that we would reopen on Monday.

Over the weekend, the back office employees and operations workers of Wall Street and the utility workers of New York City labored around the clock to make sure communications among the money center banks, brokerage firms, and exchanges were back on line. They reestablished the federal fund wire transfer system. They tested and retested all the systems on which the New York Stock Exchange relied until they were sure everything worked.

I was on the floor of the exchange that Monday morning. Lou Dobbs from CNN interviewed me and asked what I was going to do to commemorate the opening. I replied that I was going to go back to my office and buy some stock. Unfortunately I was one of the few buying that day. When the final bell rang, the market had lost almost seven hundred points. But what mattered most was that thanks to the efforts of some ten thousand people, particularly the employees of Verizon, not only did we open the market that Monday, but we processed the highest level of trade volume in the history of the New York Stock Exchange. Wall Street was back in business.

Although the Street was back overall, some of our competitors, such as Cantor Fitzgerald and Lehman Brothers, had no place to conduct major portions of their business. I instructed my staff in Weehawken to give Cantor Fitzgerald every available open desk and office we had at our disposal. I offered Lehman Brothers our redundant trading floor in New York. One of my lieutenants cautioned me that we were taxing our own capacity to the point where we were stifling our own ability to grow. One look at my expression and he immediately changed his outlook: "Sorry, Joe, I know we're in the five."

I have always believed in treating competitors with respect. Victory should come as a result of our own merits and hard work, not another's tragedy. In the days and weeks after 9/11, it was essential that the entire financial services industry work together. We had to restore not just our industry's infrastructure but the public's confidence that their money would continue to be safe in our hands. We were all in this battle together.

Prior to September 11, I had always been able to accept the self-interest of others and, in fact, use it as a motivational tool to drive behavior in the direction I needed to achieve my organization's goals. But two incidents following the attacks required me to confront, rather than accept and use, the tendency of others to work in their self-interest. I needed to ask individuals to transcend their self-interest for a greater good.

In the days following September 11, at the height of the anthrax letter scare, a suspicious envelope with white powder arrived in our mail room in Weehawken. Everyone was already sensitized to the kind of attack they'd been hearing and reading about for days. But no one really knew or understood exactly what anthrax was or how it was transmitted. Could it be treated, or was it always fatal? Did you have to touch the powder or could you get sick even by breathing near the powder? No one seemed safe; everyone from senators to network news anchors had been targeted. The appropriate protocol was initiated by the office in Weehawken, and a biohazard team in hazmat suits led my thirty mailroom employees to ambulances, which rushed them to the nearest hospital. Once the situation had been contained and our employees were examined, we learned that it would take a week to determine if the substance was anthrax.

I soon learned that the returning employees from the mailroom, some with hospital bands still on their wrists, awaiting the judgment of whether they had indeed been infected with anthrax, were being treated as lepers by the remaining 1,970 Weehawken employees. It was a time of heightened fear for everyone. The average employee did not know if anthrax was contagious and had witnessed this group of peers treated as if they were potentially infected. No memo or brochure on anthrax would temper the high emotions everyone was feeling.

I made a trip from our Manhattan headquarters to Weehawken. I went down to the mailroom, physically embraced each individual, and told them that if they had anthrax and it was contagious, then I was infected too. I guaranteed them that none of us was going to die and proceeded to spend an hour working with them to open the mail. Whether by example or through generating shame, my literal embrace of the mailroom personnel ended their pariah status. Emotions and fears calmed. The comradeship we had built at PaineWebber reasserted itself. We knew we were all in this together, and that knowledge, along with more facts and a greater understanding of the risks, was comforting.

By the end of September, the markets were securely up and running, but the whole nation was still acting like a deer caught in the headlights. No one wanted to fly anywhere, least of all to New York City. As fate would have it, the 2001 UBS PaineWebber annual meeting of branch managers from across the country had long been scheduled for early October in New York City. One afternoon I got a call from two of my lieutenants, who suggested we cancel the national managers' meeting. They told me they were getting calls from managers who were hesitant to travel. I once again headed from my midtown Manhattan office to our Weehawken, New Jersey, facility for a face-to-face meeting.

The notion of canceling the meeting violated every principle I had about patriotism, and I expressed my anger when I got to Weehawken: "Gentlemen, if you cancel that meeting, you are doing exactly what the terrorists want you to do. They want you to fear them. They want the financial system to come to a stop. You can't let these bastards win."

"But people are scared," they responded.

"Fine," I stormed back. "I'm leaving, and you have a decision to make. Cancel the meeting if you want. However, if those managers can't fly to New York, then how can you justify sending trainees to New York? The firm will have no trainees, no wholesalers, and no salesmen on the road. We will run the firm by telephone. But if the trainees, wholesalers, and salesmen can travel, the managers can travel. We ground everything, or we ground nothing."

The next morning they called to tell me they realized I was right: the meeting was still on. I recognized the understandable fear and that the families of those managers would prefer that their loved ones stay at home. However, I needed to make the point that managers were not to be treated any differently from any other employees. We had worked hard for years to create a culture in which every employee, regardless of position in the firm's hierarchy, was treated as a valuable human being. I wasn't going to change that now. Still, I didn't want to ostracize individuals. I insisted that there would be no roll calls at the meeting. If a manager chose to stay home, there wouldn't be any repercussions. The result was that 298 out of 300 managers showed up.

I felt I had to make the meeting special for the managers who had battled their fears and stepped up to the plate. A huge American flag hung on the wall in the banquet room at the Waldorf Astoria Hotel where the managers gathered. At each place setting was either a New York Police Department or Fire Department of New York hat. When I took the stage, I told the managers to put on their hats. I announced that this was the first convention to take place in New York City after 9/11 and said there was someone who wanted to say thanks. With that, I introduced Mayor Rudolph Giuliani. You can imagine the response. Those managers stayed in New York City for two days. When they left, they felt proud to work for UBS PaineWebber and proud to be Americans.

Subsequent to 9/11, I received my first experience as to how our government works—or doesn't. I received a telephone call from Governor Tom Ridge, who at the time was serving as President Bush's secretary of homeland security. He was calling on behalf of the president, asking if I would agree to become chairman of the Homeland Security Advisory Council. I said it would be a privilege. Juggling my responsibilities as chairman and CEO of UBS PaineWebber with new responsibilities chairing a governmental advisory council would be difficult. It would require a work schedule that even I found daunting and would place a tremendous burden on my lieutenants at UBS PaineWebber and my family. Corraling a dignified group of well-versed subject matter experts looked to be a challenge. However, when a former Green Beret is asked to serve by the president of the United States, he doesn't say no.

The council had among its members James Schlesinger, who had served as secretary of defense, secretary of energy, and CIA director, and Judge William Webster, who had served as director of both the CIA and the FBI. A number of such luminaries and I were given the mission to advise President Bush and Secretary Ridge on how best to make America safe.

At the first meeting of the council, I was forced to gently reprimand a senior member by suggesting that he refrain from regurgitating his past actions and instead focus on solving our current, unprecedented threat. I urged him to focus on solutions to our problem rather than conduct postmortems. When that first meeting was adjourned, one member of the council, Mayor Anthony Williams of Washington, D.C., asked to speak to me privately.

He asked, "Sir, can I give you an observation?" I responded by saying, "Anthony, the name is Joe." He said, "No, Joe, it's Sir." He went on to say that he had attended hundreds of meetings within government. This was the first one that he could recall where everyone was herded like cattle but in which the group actually got something done and how good it felt. I replied, "Well, I guess we had a good first meeting."

As a group, we continued to work on national homeland security strategy and contributed solutions on multiple issues. My single greatest frustration, however, was our inability to help facilitate the integration of more than twenty agencies employing approximately 170,000 people. Despite my best efforts and those of others on the council, we were not able to achieve our goals. Leading a $109 million one-year turnaround on Wall Street was easier than getting government officials, agencies, and bureaucracies to give up power and work together for the common good of the country.

The agencies were very siloed, and the multiple congressional appropriations committee members were focused on turf rather than solutions. I vividly recall one breakfast with a senior senator. I was seeking flexibility in deploying border patrol guards to an eventual flash point. A small percentage of the government employees within the agencies were unionized. The senator suggested to me that we couldn't move any border patrol guards to respond to an emergency unless the union selected them, the union was able to first approve the facility in which they were going to reside, and the union first investigated the available dental and medical facilities at their members' disposal in the new area. I informed the senator that he was "dead from the neck up" and that we might need to marshal the border patrol within hours. I suggested that he did not have his finger on the pulse of the American people or the patriotism expressed by union members, and as a result, he would lose his upcoming reelection effort. He did, and I thank his constituents for removing him from office.

In that story lies both the cause and the cure of much of what keeps our government from taking effective action to solve problems. It sums up the lesson I learned from the failure of our Homeland Security Advisory Council to get more done. Our elected officials are often blinded by ideology. There are some on the far, far right within our great country who believe we need an Uzi to hunt and kill a deer. Then there are those who reside on the far, far left who view the higher level of security needed to reduce our vulnerabilities as a diminution of our constitutional rights. I believe both extreme views are wrong. We are not, and should not be, in a debate about sacrificing liberty for security. We should be asking and answering how we can best secure liberty.

Many of those who govern us have lost sight of why and how they were elected. Partisan positions, turf, perks, and power granted from simple tenure rather than earned from performance are dissipating good governance. But we citizens also must share some of the blame. We should not expect congressional representatives to own a home in their own state, have a residence inside the Beltway, and put their children through college on what we pay them today. This failure propagates a system of unhealthy compromises, fosters the influence of political action committees and lobbyists, and forces our representatives to seek compensation elsewhere. It would cost a dollar a year per taxpayer to fix the economics. Shame on us if we don't.

Extreme positions, left or right, should not dictate to the majority. Unfortunately, both extremes are well organized and usually dominate our two political parties. The moderate majority is not well organized and is often an afterthought to party leaders. Hence, in the short term, the extremes of both sides drive the legislative agenda of our nation and that of other countries, at the expense of the majority. Fortunately, in a democracy, the will of the majority prevails in the long term, through the ballot box. Just as that obstructionist senator was eventually removed by his constituents, so too do American voters need to express themselves and vote for those who advocate and represent the will of the majority. All that can be found on the extremes are ideological positions. It's in the sensible middle that the pragmatic solutions are to be found.

September 11, 2001, and the months that followed tested all the leadership skills I had developed over the years. It was almost as if all the prior experiences of my life had been in preparation for the challenge I faced that day and the days that followed. Having had the privilege to lead draftee soldiers through the worst violence and warfare imaginable prepared me for the shock and fear my fellow Americans were experiencing. As CEO of a major firm on Wall Street, I shared with my peers the knowledge of what it took to get the financial markets running again and why it was necessary to ensure we were ready to reopen, or face global financial instability. Because I was one of the few CEOs experienced on the operations side of the industry, I knew firsthand just what needed to happen to keep the market working once it reopened. I uniquely understood the practical implications of our theoretical goals. September 11, 2001, was a day of tragedy that will always mark our nation's history. But I will forever be proud of how New York and Wall Street came together for this larger purpose.

My subsequent time chairing the President's Homeland Security Advisory Council served as an almost perfect counterpoint to my 9/11 experiences: I encountered the limiting effect of bureaucracy. There are times and circumstances when the status quo is too entrenched to be quickly turned around by any agent of change, no matter how skilled, motivated, and dynamic. The forceful, entrepreneurial leadership style that can work near-miracles in the military and corporate worlds does not have the same effect in Washington's corridors. Sometimes the best that can be hoped for is evolutionary, rather than revolutionary, change.

In the end, leadership in times of crisis may be more art than science. No sane individual would ever wish for a crisis. But when a crisis comes, a great leader wants to be in the middle of it. Leaders don't love crises: they love leading others through them.

"The first time we didn't listen to Joe's advice was the last time we didn't listen to Joe's advice. Joe Grano is a believer, a patriot, and above all, a great friend."

—FRANKIE VALLI AND BOB GAUDIO

Chapter Nine

CAN A LEADER PROSPER WITHOUT A MISTRESS?

Leaders do what they do because they love it. They desire the psychic income that comes from positively influencing organizations, thousands of employees, and individuals. Work is their mistress.

At the end of 2004, I left my position as chairman and CEO of UBS PaineWebber. We had completed the most successful merger in Wall Street's history, but to do so, I had to transfer almost all the capital market activities to the UBS side. To subsequently spend 100 percent of my time on the remaining consumer market side would be unfair to that management team. I decided to seek a new challenge and gracefully resigned.

One of my final decisions was to complete the branding component of the merger by relaxing the PaineWebber name fully and moving to a single brand: UBS. My decision surprised the Swiss, as they had given us the latitude to keep the associated PaineWebber name for several more years. Contemplating the ultimate fait accompli, it made no sense to me to spend the millions of dollars required to maintain a dual brand that inevitably would be moved into a single one. When I explained the rationale to my employees, they embraced the logic, understanding that the truth is never wrong. Despite the pain of seeing our 110-year-old brand slip into obscurity, they supported my decision fully.

Since my departure, the UBS brand has come under immense pressure. This has been due to mismanagement of the company's proprietary positions and several unlawful activities conducted by Swiss private bankers who entered the United States to solicit wealthy Americans with a promise of undetectable tax-avoidance schemes. Both management errors have cost the company and its shareholders, clients, and employees dearly. These mistakes have tarnished a heretofore excellent brand.

In this midst of this disaster, I wrote to the current management team and suggested they reintroduce the PaineWebber brand in the United States by selling a majority of PaineWebber to the public, a financial sponsor, and PaineWebber's financial advisors—in effect, conducting a partial employee stock option plan. The senior management of UBS did not have the courtesy to respond to my recommendation. Since that time, four of the five senior executives of UBS have been relieved of their positions.

When I left PaineWebber, I opened a new company, Centurion Holdings LLC, to advise private and public companies on how to reach the next level relative to their growth. We assist companies in developing five-year strategic plans and three-year business plans, gaining access to the capital market, and infusing new management if necessary. We do not charge monetary fees but instead receive stock, options, or warrants, giving us generally a 5 percent ownership stake in the company. The only way Centurion benefits is if the advice we provide causes the company's equity to rise in value. This puts our advice and counsel on the same side as the founders and shareholders of the company.

As I'm writing this book, Centurion is completing its fourth year in business. We are advising companies in Virginia, Washington, California, and New York, as well as in the United Kingdom and Saudi Arabia. The mandates include technology companies, security companies that provide integrated solutions in response to operational risk exposures and protection of critical infrastructure, and even a green company that provides master planning for environmental land and building development. In addition, Centurion has founded three companies: Visible Technologies, which has become a significant player in the Internet-based social media space; 1–800PackRat, a national franchise that provides mobile storage similar to PODS; and Ecological Development, a new company dealing with the green movement that has tremendous momentum. Seventeen companies are now in our portfolio.

Such a diverse array of industries and companies has validated what I had often preached: that management and leadership skills are fungible. If you take the time to learn the value proposition of a company—usually sixty days of due diligence— and you familiarize yourself with the customized jargon of the industry, your managerial approach can remain the same. Apply the universal tenets of management—planning, leading, organizing, controlling—stay client-centric and solution based, and you can dramatically influence the outcome.

There are two major differences between advising a company and being the CEO: you cannot exercise your leadership skills, other than advising the company's management team; and you are not in a position to execute a plan or a strategy because you are not managing the company day to day.

Without question, addressing the challenges facing these companies in need provides significant intellectual stimulus. However, it does not provide a seasoned leader with the psychic income that stimulates his or her very being. You are no longer standing in front of an audience of thousands, getting them to drink the Kool-Aid and go over the hill. I still miss it.

Initially you miss the so-called CEO perks, such as a private plane or staff who react immediately to your beck and call. Those perks become diluted with time, but the psychic income void never leaves.

I have witnessed this phenomenon with many retired or displaced CEOs. You can sense the void in their lives and the impact on their demeanors. Many of them, who have not compensated for the influx of downtime or leisure time, begin to age physically. It is also a common critique from the spouses of disengaged CEOs and leaders that they have a propensity to direct activities in the home that they had delegated to their spouses when they were working seventy-hour workweeks. As the saying goes, "For better or worse . . . but not for lunch."

Leaders can play only so much golf, can vacation for only so long, and are accustomed to having their directives followed without question. They need to supplement this newly acquired environment with activities that can at least challenge their minds. My outlet is Centurion Holdings.

One of the positives of having some success under your belt is that you can be more selective about those with whom you choose to do business and with the type of businesses in which you choose to engage. Although the Centurion portfolio traverses seventeen different companies, domiciled in six different industries, they all met common selection criteria.

At Centurion, we apply three basic rules.

First, we have to respect the value proposition of the potential client company. We have to like what the company does for a living.

Second, we need to convince ourselves that the opportunity exists for Centurion to earn $10 million from our equity position if we are successful in bringing the company to the next level. We accept that not every company in our portfolio will succeed. However, we must believe that the opportunity is there for every company we take on as a client. It is analogous to the hourglass effect I wrote about earlier in this book when describing my early career as a stockbroker. Centurion is in the middle of a similar hourglass and is relegated to being somewhat discretionary relative to its choices. Time is an enemy, as every client wants face time with us.

Third, and perhaps most important, the senior management team of any company we take on as a client must be, what I call, "AF," which means asshole free! Throughout my career I have been forced to deal with my share of assholes. With the flexibility that my success has afforded me, I can choose whom I wish to deal with. It is refreshing to see the reaction from a CEO of a small company when I articulate the three rules. Of course, we have already made our assessment prior to articulating the rules, but the client CEO doesn't know that. Often

when we get to the AF rule, the individual responds by promis-
ing that he or she is not an asshole.

My success has done more than give me the ability to
avoid assholes; it has also given me the chance to help friends.
There are few things more satisfying than being able to help
those close to you when they're in need. For me, investing in
friends has always paid off emotionally. Sometimes it can even
pay off financially.

Some thirty years ago, Frankie Valli and the Four Seasons
were hired to entertain our best brokers and their spouses at a
Merrill Lynch recognition trip. Subsequent to their performance, Frankie Valli hosted a cocktail party with our management team. For whatever reason, Frankie and I connected. I
imagine it was partially due to the fact that we both grew up
on the street and share an Italian heritage. I did not think
much about that evening until six months later when Frankie
Valli, Bob Gaudio (his famous partner-songwriter), and a
group of five of their business associates arrived at my office
unannounced. Frankie said, "Joe, I'm sorry to just show up on
your doorstep, but we need financial advice and you are the
only person I trust." I was surprised by his comment considering I had known him for perhaps all of two hours.

The advice he was seeking was my opinion of a business
transaction between Frankie Valli and the Four Seasons and the
group represented by the five business associates. The proposal
was for the Four Seasons to jointly build and own a recording
studio at a cost of $5 million. After reviewing the proposal, I
dismissed the external group so I could speak with Frankie and
Bob alone. I informed them that they should disassociate
themselves from the external group, as I believed the proposal

to be "egregious," and that they were being taken advantage of. Unfortunately, they did not take my advice and ultimately lost several million dollars.

A year later, we rehired Frankie Valli and the Four Seasons to entertain at another broker recognition trip. I was sitting in the front row when Frankie walked onto the front stage. He grabbed the microphone and said, "Ladies and gentlemen. All of my life people have told me what to do. Only one person has told me what *not* to do, and I will never not listen to him again: your president, Joe Grano." His remarks both surprised and humbled me.

I have been a close friend to both Frankie Valli and Bob Gaudio ever since. I have spent hundreds of hours giving them friendly advice and have even agreed to be a trustee of their respective estates. Throughout the years, I have done so out of friendship and have never charged them for my time or expenses.

In 2006, Frankie and Bob showcased a new musical at the La Jolla Playhouse in California, written by Marshall Brickman (of *Annie Hall* fame) and the superb playwright Rick Elice. The director was Des McAnuff. The show, *Jersey Boys,* shares the life and success of Frankie Valli and the Four Seasons. It describes how they began as a group of young, hardened wise guys, singing in local joints around Newark, New Jersey. The show exposes the criminal elements influencing the group, and how they ultimately broke through the difficult environment in which they were raised. The story exemplifies the American dream, nostalgia, and the ultimate return you can achieve from hard work and maximizing your unique talent. At the height of their career, the band had more than thirty gold records and was the only American singing group to compete successfully with The Beatles.

I knew I would invest in the show out of friendship alone. Still, I had mixed emotions as I traveled to California to attend the grand opening, as I was concerned that Californians were much more closely aligned with the Beach Boys genre than the more East Coast sound of the Four Seasons. To my astonishment, the La Jolla Playhouse was sold out and the show's run had been extended three times to accommodate the demand for tickets. I absolutely loved the show. I was thrilled that everyone in the audience, from people my age to teenagers, seemed to respond to the music with the same enthusiasm. I felt like I did when I was a kid hanging out in The Avenue in Hartford and first heard Frankie and the boys sing "Sherry." It was incredible to see the whole audience singing along to the soundtrack of my teenage years.

The lead producer of the show, the Dodger Group, had produced several successful Broadway plays in the past. They were heavily dependent on a single individual to finance their endeavors. As fate would have it, after a string of losing productions, their financier had decided to withdraw from the business of investing in plays. In order to bring *Jersey Boys* to Broadway, the Dodger Group now needed to raise $7.5 million. At the time of the grand opening, they had commitments for only half of the money, including my own investment. Since they had no existing network of investors due to their past reliance on one man, they approached me for advice. I agreed to join the production team to provide them with advice and strategy. As a limited investor, I would receive my initial investment back and share in 50 percent of any profits. As a producer, I could also get a share of the producer's profits. Of course, for anyone to get any return required the play to be successful. Since eight out of ten Broadway plays lose money, the odds would have been better taking my money to Vegas.

Thanks to divine intervention and all those years of friendship, I am now a producer of one of the most successful shows in the world, *Jersey Boys.* It has turned out to be one of my most successful investments, and more important, it has created two new generations of fans for the music of Frankie Valli and the Four Seasons. It has become a phenomenon. It's the only show I know of that has men telling other men they have to go see it. My two dear friends Frankie and Bob will never have to worry about retirement. I have been crowned with a Midas touch reputation, that while amusing, could more adequately be described as being in the right place at the right time for the past thirty years.

In the midst of our current economic downturn, *Jersey Boys* is still establishing records everywhere it plays. It has been the number one play in New York, Chicago, Las Vegas, London, and Toronto. There's one traveling company that sets a record in every playhouse it visits, and another production is opening in Melbourne, Australia.

Despite my personal success with *Jersey Boys,* Centurion and every other American business has faced extraordinary challenges in 2009. Since the beginning of the demise of the credit markets, many start-ups and even some mature companies have experienced difficulty in raising capital for growth. When venture capital companies move in unison to deeply discount valuations, the founders of businesses looking for capital are faced with the prospect of losing control. Their founders' equity becomes subservient to new capital that generally receives preferred status. As a result, the founder's equity ownership gets heavily diluted. When the initial public offering market dries up like this, young growth companies lose an important avenue for capital to fuel their growth.

The lack of the initial public offerings also hurts companies such as Centurion because regardless of the theoretical value of our positions, they cannot be monetized or liquefied. Currently we find ourselves in an environment where the "cash is king" philosophy is dominant. Banks, forced to defend their balance sheets in order to remain solvent, are unwilling to lend. The precipitous decline of both the stock and bond markets has shattered investor confidence and resulted in a massive diminution of buying power. Finally, the sacred cow represented by our real estate holdings, our homes, the values of which we thought could never go down, has already declined an average of 30 percent. Our national misery meter is scoring off the charts. Something has to be done.

"Great leaders have vision, they have a commitment to make things happen, and they take action to deliver on their vision. That's what Joe's all about. Joe has a belief that every child deserves to succeed. He is very purposeful, he is very passionate, and he is very powerful in what he does. He uses his mind, he uses his energy, and he uses the great values and spirit to make things happen."

—PAULA GAVIN, FORMER PRESIDENT OF
THE YMCA OF GREATER NEW YORK

Chapter Ten

QUEEN FOR A DAY

When I was a boy, I recall the excitement when my father brought home our first television set. It was encased in a piece of furniture and had a twelve-inch black and white screen. That transformation, the ability of a working-class family to watch a program on a television set, was as much a paradigm shift as the Internet has been for society today.

One of the programs I remember watching on that old set was *Queen for a Day*. It was a perversely entertaining show. As I recall, a group of contestants would compete with each other by articulating just how difficult their lives were ("My left arm is atrophying, my husband left me penniless, and my son is very ill"). After telling their tale of woe, the audience would clap, and the volume of the audience's clapping would then be measured by a "misery meter": the worse the circumstances and the sadder the story, the louder the applause. The contestant whose tale of misery inspired the most applause was named "Queen for a Day," and given a variety of prizes. If the misery meter climbed to 9 or 10, the person might even win a refrigerator.

When I pick up a newspaper or turn on a financial news-cast today, I am reminded of that program and the misery meter. There's an endless litany of bad news, a proclivity to attack anyone with a high profile, and stories of a bureaucracy that functions on indecent compromise: not an effort to find a middle ground, but a selfish willingness to trade a vote for *your* pet project if you vote for *mine*.

These are perhaps the most difficult economic and polit-ical times I have experienced. I do not believe, however, that as Americans, we should accept a misery meter culture, nor should we be applauding the next insolvent company or failed government program. We and our leaders should be focusing on solutions that will restore the economic and political stabil-ity we wish to bequeath to our children. This will not come from burying a hypothetical grant of $30 million to study a white mouse or an earthworm in a legislative economic relief bill, any more than it will come from pretending that the poli-cies of the past are sufficient to deal with an unprecedented cri-sis. It comes from our new president and the American people insisting on a culture that focuses on solutions and dreams rather than scapegoats and the misery meter.

If President Obama were to have a monthly fireside chat with the American people and exposed a pork barrel spending bill or a legislative hypocrisy while simultaneously showing a picture of the sponsoring senator or congressperson in the lower right corner of our TV screen, this nonsense would end forever.

Certainly these are difficult times, but are they any more difficult than the circumstances immigrants faced when they passed through Ellis Island? Are they more difficult than what Americans confronted during the Great Depression? Are they as hard as the times people lived in while fighting World War II? The solution will come not out of the adversity we face but out of how we face the adversity. Preceding generations dealt with adversity by optimistically seeking solutions. What we need is a dream meter rather than a misery meter.

It would certainly be appropriate to define our current economy as being in crisis. We could add to our own economic crisis a global economic crisis. We might also agree that despite the interdependencies all nations of the world have with each other, there is also a political crisis driven by ideology, religion, and war. That leads to plenty of applause for our collective misery meter. But I'll play "king for a day" and explore ways we can face these challenges and earn applause for our dream meter.

Take the case of social security. Our looming problem is actually a simple one: too few workers supporting too many retirees. When President Franklin D. Roosevelt introduced social security, it was perhaps the most astute political event of its time. The value proposition was providing a safety net to our citizens when they stopped working. When social security was introduced, average life expectancy was sixty-four years of age. In essence, not many people were going to live to collect benefits. At that time, more than twenty workers were contributing to the fund for every living recipient. Today life expectancies are approaching eighty years of age, and fewer than four workers contribute for each recipient. This ratio is unsustainable, and predictions are that social security will be theoretically bankrupt by 2030.

If our government officials didn't represent ideological poles and instead took the true pulse of the American people, they would see there's a solution. The average American over age forty-five feels entitled to social security benefits, based on his or her years of contributions. Americans under forty-five years of age don't believe social security will be there for them. That's a proverbial Mason-Dixon line of demography. I believe our government should grandfather today's social security benefits for all Americans who are age forty-five and older, commencing January 1, 2010. All Americans under age forty-five on that date should have to work until at least seventy-two years of age to receive full benefits. This is no great sacrifice: they are going to live longer than their predecessors. Besides, they don't like forced retirement. In exchange for the delay, they should be allowed to double their individual retirement account (IRA) contributions so the accrued benefits of tax deferrals will offset any benefits lost from having to wait to collect. Americans, I believe, would perceive this kind of compromise solution as fair. Critics might correctly point out that the poor under age forty-five might not be able to afford to double their IRA contributions. However, the issues of poverty and social security are separate. There is no magic pill to solve all ills; we need to focus on our large problems one at a time.

When dealing with a crisis, as I have suggested throughout this book, you must focus on solutions, not postmortems. You should look at the past only to provide information that may help in finding a solution. That's especially valuable when confronting large, unprecedented crisis, such as the financial storm that struck the economy in 2008.

It's inarguable that our nation has entered into the worst financial crisis since the Great Depression. Wall Street, for all intents and purposes, has disappeared. Goodbye Bear Stearns,

Lehman Brothers, and Merrill Lynch. The Bear and Merrill were purchased respectively by JPMorgan Chase and Bank of America. Lehman Brothers was forced into bankruptcy, which resulted in an unprecedented shock wave attacking worldwide credit markets. AIG, the largest insurer in the world, was nationalized by the government, and Washington Mutual (WAMU) was sold to JPMorgan Chase. Wachovia Bank was forced into a fire sale and was subsequently purchased by Wells Fargo. The two remaining bulge bracket investment houses, Goldman Sachs and Morgan Stanley, converted to bank holding companies in order to have access to the federal funds window. By the time this book reaches stores, it's likely even more famous names in the financial services industry will have disappeared or been transformed.

The financial shock waves have crossed the Atlantic and Pacific, permeating the European Union, United Kingdom, Russia, Japan, and emerging countries such as China. Central banks around the world have responded with mass infusions of hundreds of billions of dollars in order to provide liquidity. Banks, corporations, investment houses, insurance companies, and hedge funds were shocked to see a precipitous decline in the value of their balance sheets, a shutdown of previously approved credit lines, misunderstood counterparty risks, margin calls, and credit default swaps that could not be honored. (A counterparty risk is a trade in which you have to bear the full risk of the party you traded with. If that party suffers losses from unrelated investments, it may not be able to fulfill its obligations to you. And if you suffer losses from other unrelated investments, you may not be able to fulfill your obligations to the other party. A margin call is a demand by a broker that an investor who has bought securities with borrowed funds deposit additional funds so the account is brought up to the balance required by the broker's policies. A credit default swap is a derivative contract, similar to insurance, in which a buyer pays premiums to a seller and in return receives a payoff if an underlying financial instrument defaults. Unlike insurance, the seller doesn't need to be regulated or to maintain reserves to pay off buyers, and the buyer doesn't need to own the underlying security or even suffer a loss from the default.) Words and phrases such as *bailout, excess executive compensation, lack of regulation, overleverage,* and *nationalization* have dominated the news. How could our society, and other societies around the world, go from one of the most prosperous decades in history to the brink of Armageddon literally overnight?

The finger pointing started as soon as the extent of the crisis became clear. "It was Wall Street's fault: the greed of those CEOs knows no bounds." "The American public is to blame for living beyond its means for decades." "No, it's the culmination of the Republican belief in unregulated markets." "Wrong. It's because the Democrats pushed Freddie Mac and Fannie Mae to make loans to people who should never have bought homes." "Greenspan should have known what would happen. He's not as smart as we thought." "Bernanke, for all his expertise on the Great Depression, just didn't move quickly enough." We witnessed the typical "who did it?" response by most CEOs, politicians, and government bureaucrats. But this classic search for scapegoats does nothing to help and only makes it more difficult to develop and unite behind a solution.

Hindsight is always twenty-twenty. Knowing the outcome makes it easy to critique the actions of all the major players in the crisis, from the CEOs of Wall Street firms, insurers and banks, the members of Bush administration, and the leaders of Congress, to the two presidential candidates in 2008. Obviously this was not one of our nation's finest hours. There were no "profiles in courage" moments. That said, I don't believe we witnessed a failure in leadership as much as we experienced a financial perfect storm.

In 1999 our Congress directed Fannie Mae, Freddie Mac, and the Department of Housing and Urban Development to lower credit standards in order to provide subprime mortgages. The intent was to provide loans to Americans who otherwise could not afford to buy their own homes. The consequence of this mandate was the development of a new segment of home owners who, in many cases, were not properly vetted as to their ability to maintain their mortgage payments. Exacerbating the lack of credit-worthiness was a group of predatory lenders who enticed this segment of our population with teaser-like adjustable-note mortgages. These loans started out with interest rates as low as 3 percent in order to keep the monthly mortgage payments low. The theory behind this lending was that as long as housing prices continued to escalate, the lenders would be secure, even if the borrowers were unable to meet their obligations when the mortgage interest rate reset as high as 8.5 percent. As long as the lender could foreclose on a home worth more than the mortgage amount due, who cared?

After this unprecedented growth in subprime loans, our nation experienced the first major attack on our shores since Pearl Harbor: the attacks of September 11, 2001. Our economy and the markets froze due to the shock of being so vulnerable, the expectation of additional attacks, and the resulting buildup of our military complex and military budget. Alan Greenspan and the Federal Reserve reacted by precipitously dropping interest rates in order to jump-start our slumping economy. Now we had an environment of lower credit standards and cheap money.

Not too long after 9/11, the major investment banks on Wall Street solicited and received permission from the Securities and Exchange Commission to increase the leverage of their balance sheets. Several firms' notional footings went from a leverage ratio of eight-to-one to a ratio as high as forty-to-one, making them far less secure. Add to the unparalleled jump in leverage ratios the lack of transparency caused by offshore special-purpose vehicles, which in turn screened to some degree this building mountain of mortgage-backed securities, credit default swaps, and untested contra party risk. (Special-purpose vehicles, made notorious by Enron, are subsidiary companies formed to acquire and finance specific assets, whose structures and legal status make the obligations secure whatever the health of the parent company. Although they were originally designed to finance large projects without risking the whole company, they could also be used to hide liabilities.)

The consequence of cheap money and overleverage fueled record earnings at investment banks, banks, and insurance companies. Many CEOs felt compelled to match this model or face deteriorating earnings relative to their competitors, leading to a decline in their company's stock price, which in turn could cost them their jobs. A herd mentality ensued. If you didn't keep up with Joneses or if you missed your "consensus" earnings by even a penny, the talking heads on the financial programs and the institutional investors would crush your stock price. There was literally no discussion by reporters, research analysts, or ratings agencies around the quality of a firm's balance sheet or its firm's earnings. The result was an investment culture in which you either played or you paid.

Now, in the midst of this environment, picture a hypothetical Ivy League M.B.A. working at an investment bank. Armed with a laptop, our investment banker creates the next innovative security using algorithms to assess the potential value of various tranches of the same security by stripping, dipping, flipping, slicing, and dicing a much more complex security. Then wrap this highly leveraged, complex security holding with a series of synthetic derivatives to hedge the bet. Meanwhile, another hypothetical Ivy League M.B.A., this one working at a rating agency, buys into the conceptual computer model and subsequent hedges created by the investment banker counterpart and assigns the security an AAA rating.

Relative to these exotic products, the traditional CEO was simply not as smart as the two M.B.A.s who designed and rated the security. But those two brilliant M.B.A.s didn't understand that there is no hedge when there is no liquidity in the market because the underlying security divorces itself from the derivative. Despite the leverage and concentration, the CEO rationalized his or her need to keep up with the Joneses and any innate discomfort by saying, "Well, it is AAA rated."

Severe cracks in the credit and real estate markets began surfacing. The realization of overleveraged, concentrated mortgage-backed positions, difficult-to-price securities, counterparty risk, falling real estate prices, a big jump in foreclosures, and an absolute drying up of liquidity crashed the credit and stock markets. Bear Stearns melted, and a mad scramble ensued to begin deleveraging, reduce concentrated positions, and raise cash. Unfortunately, the combination of no liquidity and a massive rush for the exit caused a heretofore orderly market to become dysfunctional.

As the contributors to this perfect storm reacted to defend their actions, they served only to compound the problem. The rating agencies lowered their ratings of the products and the firms that owned them. The traders rushed to sell at any price to salvage their balance sheets. Auditors and the Securities and Exchange Commission were armed with an accounting rule (FASB 157) that forced the firms to mark the value of their security holdings based on the prices at which they could sell the security. In an illiquid, dysfunctional market, sales prices are artificially low because the only buyers are vulture funds and hedge funds. Those that were "long" the securities faced massive write-downs and quick asset sales in order to raise cash. These same firms became subject to having established credit lines cancelled and were forced to identify subsidiaries or divisions of their company that they could sell quickly. The journalists who had failed to see the storm coming became doomsayers once it hit in an effort to salvage their reputations. As the markets continued to deteriorate, so did the financial conditions of what once were considered great firms.

Federal Reserve chairman Ben Bernanke and Treasury Secretary Henry Paulson responded to the crisis swiftly. They interceded in facilitating mergers between the strong financial institutions and those that were weakened beyond repair. Unfortunately, in the case of Lehman Brothers, they opted to let the firm fail. The thought process during that second week of September 2008 was that counterparties had ample time to react to Lehman Brothers's problems. Furthermore, public opinion had reached a crescendo of outcry over the perceived "bailout" of Wall Street, which made the bankruptcy of Lehman Brothers politically expedient. Given the shock wave that this bankruptcy caused, I believe it would have been much more prudent to assist a buyer in purchasing Lehman Brothers. Of course, hindsight is always twenty-twenty. No one, not even those of us who went through the crash of 1987, had experienced anything like the crisis of 2008. It is unproductive to retrospectively criticize the tactics of those steering the economy through uncharted waters.

That said, there is one element of crisis leadership in which it appears that all our national leaders came up short and from which we can learn in our continued efforts to battle this crisis: a failure in communications. It is unfortunate that our political leadership in the administration and Congress, our business leaders, and the media positioned the efforts to stabilize the crisis as a bailout. If it was portrayed as an economic stabilization plan rather than a bailout, and if the importance of the plan to the health of Main Street, not just Wall Street, was clearly explained, we might have been able to stem the bleeding sooner.

It is still too early to judge the effectiveness of the government's $700 billion Troubled Assets Relief Program (TARP). Its ultimate success may be not as a recovery tool but as a means to prevent a crisis from turning into a catastrophe. Without TARP, things would have been worse. Pumping in liquidity and lessening the burden of mispriced assets on the balance sheets of corporations and banks should result in an eventual normalization of our credit markets.

But this is only the first leg of a three-legged solution. The TARP plan alone will not mitigate an economic recession. Worldwide economies must continue to deleverage, and consumption, the major component of the U.S. gross domestic product (GDP), will continue to decline until the fear abates and real estate prices end their downward spiral. That will require the other two legs of our solution stool.

President Obama needs to focus on reducing the record levels of foreclosures by keeping people in their homes and develop programs that can help mitigate the decline in real estate prices. When you peel away the multiple layers of complexity, the root causes of declining mortgage-backed securities are foreclosures and falling real estate prices.

Hundreds of thousands of homes are now valued at less than the mortgage owed. As the owners of these homes experience a major jump in monthly payments because their adjustable rates reset at a higher rate, many of them realize that they not only have lost their down payment but wonder why they should continue to pay for a home they feel they no longer own. Too often this results in the homeowner telling the bank to take the keys, and we see a new sign in front of the home announcing a "short sale" in which the proceeds don't need to meet the balance owed on the mortgage. For those hard-working home owners, it is the end of their American dream.

This phenomenon is adding downside pressure to an already declining real estate market. A foreclosed home or a short sale drags down the resale value of neighbors' homes as well. To stop this negative spiral, we need to find a way to keep the family in the home, with an affordable mortgage, and preclude the next foreclosure or short sale. Otherwise our current economic problems will become even more severe. The lifeblood of every community in America is property taxes. If we don't address this issue, every municipality, county, and town will face severe budget deficits as their property tax revenues decline.

How can we reduce the levels of foreclosures and mitigate the decline in real estate prices? Here is my idea for the kind of program our new president should launch. I call it the American Dream Mortgage.

Let's start with a typical scenario. A family, with both spouses working and an income of under $100,000, buys a home for $350,000 with a down payment of $50,000 and a thirty-year variable rate mortgage with an initial teaser rate of 3 percent. Their initial monthly payment was $1,264.81. Then their mortgage rate resets to 8 percent and their monthly payment climbs to $2,201.29. The couple struggles desperately to make this new payment, while also being burdened by the property taxes that have risen since they purchased the home. The issuing bank is indifferent to their plight and may actually have already securitized the original mortgage. The couple realizes that their home is worth less today than the original purchase price. They are told that in today's real estate market, they can reasonably expect to sell their home for only $250,000. All these realities converge, and the couple is faced with the prospect of selling their home for less than they owe; they have lost their down payment of $50,000 and face bankruptcy. They decide to tell the bank to take the keys and foreclose.

Here's one possible solution. Refinance the $300,000 mortgage with a Federal Housing Administration (FHA) mortgage at a 5 percent interest rate, amortized over fifty years. This special American Dream Mortgage would be available to couples earning under $250,000 a year or individuals earning under $125,000. The difference between the current appraised value of the home and the amount of the refinanced FHA mortgage cannot exceed $50,000. For example, if the home in our example is appraised at $230,000, the new mortgage cannot exceed $280,000. This mortgage should also be assumable for seven years, meaning a new buyer can assume the fifty-year, 5 percent mortgage if they buy the house within that seven-year period. If, during that seven-year period, the house is sold for more than the mortgage, the profits are split fifty-fifty between the seller and the federal government. This rewards American taxpayers for helping their neighbors in need. If the house is sold after the seventh year, the buyer will have to secure a conventional mortgage. During this seven-year period, the refinanced mortgage subsidy is reflected on the couple's credit score, similar to a bankruptcy. This mortgage subsidy by the FHA is similar to the assumable Veterans Administration mortgage available to servicemen and servicewomen when they returned from Vietnam.

Let's look at the impact such a plan would have:

- The couple's current monthly mortgage payment of $2,201.29 would drop to $1,362.42, very close to their original teaser rate payment of $1,264.81 a month.

- The fact that the 5 percent, fifty-year FHA mortgage is assumable for the first seven years would drive the value of the home up closer to the $300,000 value set at the time of the initial mortgage.

- The couple wouldn't walk away from their home and mortgage, precluding another foreclosure, which typically results in a loss to the issuer of $120,000 and drives all real estate prices in the neighborhood down.

- The issuer of the refinanced mortgage would have a total risk of only $21,000 because the FHA would guarantee 93 percent of the mortgage (7 percent of $300,000 equals $21,000). This would allow community banks to reprice the mortgages on their balance sheets upward, releasing capital for additional lending. And the bank avoids potential losses from foreclosures.

- Communities throughout America would benefit by stabilizing real estate prices, which in turn stabilizes property taxes.

Limiting the mortgage to couples with an income of under $250,000 and individuals under $125,000, and having the mortgage subsidy reflected for seven years on the borrowers' credit report, will make sure the program focuses on those with the most need, limit borrowers' future borrowing capacity to keep them from replacing this debt with another debt, and deter individuals who don't need the subsidy from applying.

I believe a plan like this would have a positive impact on the current decline in real estate. It assists couples who are in trouble and whose American dream has been crushed. It could benefit their neighbors as well by precluding a foreclosure that will drag their home's value down with the foreclosed house next door. The assumable mortgage will cause the home to rise in value, with a possible outcome that it again will be worth more than the mortgage. If a profit is realized, the seller shares it with the Treasury, which rewards all Americans for assisting those in need. Banks, insurance companies, and mortgage holders would all benefit by turning a nonperforming loan into a performing loan. And it can help all American communities. All municipalities rely on property taxes. If we do not address the decline of real estate prices, which reduces property taxes, which in turn puts all city and town budgets at risk, we face a national debacle. A program like the American Dream Mortgage can restore our economy and confidence in America.

In past recessions, government policy encouraged more spending: "Spend your way out" was the mantra. Our current economy is suffering from deflation and budget deficits that are historically high as percentages of GDP. There simply isn't any money to spend. We need stabilization within our credit and real estate markets. In the coming months, it is very likely that our economy will also have to absorb a wave of credit card defaults and a dramatic increase in unemployment due to massive deleveraging within corporate America. Our national economic priorities should be market liquidity, price stabilization, curtailing foreclosures, and fostering employment. We must understand that there will be no "do-all" cocktail to drink. Regardless of the programs that the Obama administration and the federal government deploy, they must keep those four priorities in front of any agenda.

We can spur employment with a comprehensive new energy policy. We can assist market liquidity by facilitating consolidation within the banking industry. We can help to stabilize pricing by creating a new protocol for marking to market illiquid securities. And we can help end the downward spiral of real estate prices and foreclosures by adopting plans such as the American Dream Mortgage. My ultimate message in dealing with this crisis is, "Don't bet against America."

When assessing the global economic and political situation, we must understand that while today's short-term financial crisis requires immediate attention, there is also a looming global cultural and demographic crisis that demands not just our long-term attention but action. We need national leaders who appreciate that multiple crises can't be tackled serially; they must be addressed simultaneously.

Sometime in the not-too-distant future, passports will disappear, and an even larger flow of humanity will cross our borders. As managers, coworkers, and neighbors, we will have to deal with cultural diversity issues the likes of which our society can't even imagine. Three out of every five replacement workers in the near future are today's minorities. Tomorrow's business leaders will be responsible for making this blend of cultures work if we are to not just weather today's perfect storm but continue as the world's leading economic power.

Let me share with you an interesting study conducted by the Dilenschneider Group some years ago. Although some of the ratios have since changed, the message remains the same. It took the world's population and shrunk it to a microcosm of precisely one hundred people. With all existing human ratios remaining the same, the profile of our one-hundred-person, all-world village emerged as follows:

- There are fifty-seven Asians, twenty-one Europeans, fourteen people from North and South America, and eight people from Africa living in our village.
- Fifty-one are female and forty-nine are male.

- Seventy are nonwhite and thirty are white.

- Sixty-six are non-Christian and thirty-four are Christian.

- Eighty live in substandard housing.

- Seventy cannot read.

- Half suffer from malnutrition.

- Seventy-five have never made a telephone call.

- Fewer than one is on the Internet.

- Only one has a college degree.

- Most important, half of the entire village's wealth would be in the hands of six people. All six would be citizens of the United States.

As democratic and capitalistic values are embraced and demanded by the people of the planet, they will look to the most successful people in our village: you, America's future leaders. The democratization of Eastern Europe brought on a euphoric expectation of a new capitalist consumer bloc. Reality was different. Freedom has often brought with it the rebirth of religious and ethnic genocidal conflict (just look at the Balkans). The cost to West Germany of integration with East Germany was perhaps four times greater than anticipated. This new freedom comes with a price that the already free world must help bear, one that will need to be borne by tomorrow's generation as well as today's. The freeing world will look to the already free world for support and guidance, and perhaps even protection.

In providing that support, guidance, and protection, we will need to avoid a uniquely American bad habit: we expect people in other countries to follow our logic train, think the way we think, value what we value. Consider Iraq. Even if we all would have made the same decision to attack Iraq, given the circumstantial evidence of weapons of mass destruction, how could we believe that a pure form of American democracy could be imposed on a country without a middle class?

There are twenty-two countries in the Arab League, and we Americans are enamored by the riches we believe they enjoy due to their oil resources. At the time the attacks of 9/11 occurred, the cumulative GDP of those twenty-two countries was $531 billion. The GDP of just Spain at that time was $596 billion. There are approximately 282 million people living in that part of the world. One out of five of them cannot read or write. Half of all women there cannot read or write. Twenty-five percent of the population there lives on two dollars a day. Fifty-one percent of adults and 45 percent of youth there would emigrate if they could.

I have great respect for Bernard Lewis, a professor at Princeton University, and his views on the Middle East and our current war on terrorism. He describes the United States as a nation divided by religious groups. Islam, he contends, is a religion divided by nations. I believe *that* difference alone creates a hugely different perspective. He also contends that when Osama bin Laden talks of the suffering experienced by Muslims over the past eighty years, he is referring to the foreign occupation of Constantinople and the fall of the Ottoman Empire in 1918. You and I don't still walk around saying, "Remember the Alamo," but bin Laden and the radical extremists he leads do remember the end of Muslim dominance. To his radicals, we are the supreme infidels due to our success, our democracy, and our civil liberties. They wish to destroy all infidels represented by any and all democratic countries. He and his followers divide the world literally into the House of Islam and the House of War. Because of that radical thinking, we were a target on September 11, and we, as well as other democracies, will continue to be targets.

Because of the lack of a middle class in many parts of the world, there will continue to be those who are susceptible to the false promises and appeals of a charismatic, extremist, religious zealot or revolutionary. As Adlai Stevenson so astutely noted years ago, the poor of the world are consumed by rising expectations. (Stevenson was governor of Illinois, ran unsuccessfully as the Democratic candidate for president twice, and served as President John F. Kennedy's ambassador to the United Nations.) They own or have access to a radio or television. They witness a much higher standard of living in other parts of the world, and they want it now. It is not an acceptable option for them to go from A to B to C to D. They want to go directly from A to D, even if it takes a revolution. As evidence, look at the number of revolutions within Latin America in the past hundred years. Once you mix these given truths with religion or radical fanaticism, you can no longer debate or rationalize or compromise with them. Zealots and radicals do not think the way we do.

The long-term solution begins with accepting the facts, the truth. It won't work to think in a vertical manner, that is, as if everyone should think American. Leaders of today and tomorrow must think horizontally. You will need to be sensitive to the different cultures of the world and to their different ways of thinking. And please don't believe that the peoples of the world agree with the radicals or the zealots. They do not. Encourage a better choice. Demonstrate a better opportunity.

Transfer your technology and capital to create a better standard of living around the globe. Then, and only then, will the majority of the world be able to contain the radical minority.

This central leadership challenge of tomorrow won't be just an exercise in foreign aid. Business leaders in the future will need to deal with a much more diverse employee base as minorities replace the old guard and an old guard that, because of extended life spans, doesn't want to retire. Think of a society that resembles a barbell. At one end of the barbell are the new, young, diverse entrants fueled by the largest increase in births and the most massive immigration to the United States from the end of the twentieth century through today. At the other end of the barbell is the fastest-growing segment of our population: the aging baby boomers. Are we prepared as a society to deal with and manage this demographic shift? Have our managers been given even a minute of training in how to deal with a minority, diverse, aging workforce?

You, as a manager and leader of today and tomorrow, need to be more proactive if we as a nation are to survive and prosper. The vitality of our businesses will be directly commensurate with our ability to nurture the vitality of our youth. It is the vitality of the young that got us to where we are as a nation in the first place: those aspiring young immigrants like my grandparents spawned succeeding generations, like my parents and me, who embraced the opportunities that our country afforded them. The new generation, native born and immigrant, will fulfill the jobs of the new economy. We have the human resources here today.

You, as a business leader, must inculcate these new citizens in your respective firms and prepare them to share, maintain, and expand our legacy. They can smooth our success in a global economy as they speak more than a hundred different languages. They can educate us, define for us, and help us penetrate the immense economic blocs represented by varying ethnic groups. These new citizens are today, and will remain, the predominant human resource that must be assimilated into those sectors of the economy demanding educated, intensive workforces: health services, business services, social services, engineering, and management and related services. They are here, waiting for the opportunity that we, as employers, taxpayers, and fellow citizens, can grant them.

How can we as business leaders address this cultural and demographic crisis and take advantage of the opportunity it offers? We can manage the change and lead by using one of the leadership skills I've written about in this book: by showing that we value individual human beings.

We need to engage in the debate for revitalizing our city and state school systems. We need to support the needed increases in salaries for our teachers, professors, and college presidents, which embarrassingly lag other industries. We need to join with educational institutions in an effort to define the needs of business and the needs of the new generation.

We need to establish diversity efforts within all firms. Champion a diverse employee base at all levels of your organization. Shift from a defensive posture, relative to government regulations and legislation, to a proactive, opportunistic posture that suggests that diversity and respect in the workplace are good business.

We need to review and, where necessary, modify archaic employee policies. Reevaluate flex hours, cafeteria benefit plans, and dress codes in the light of today's realities. Learn what is important to a Hispanic, an Asian, an African, a South Asian, and teach it to your managers.

We need to support city and state government initiatives in attracting and keeping business in local communities. Evaluate tax and training subsidies with an intermediate and long-term view. Evaluate their economic contribution to your city and state in totality and become a voice of reason that can respond to the emotional reactions so often expressed in the press.

We need to become an example of what should be by leading and encouraging change. Mentor the young, develop the new while being sensitive to the needs of the old, and be totally intolerant of any remaining pockets of bigotry left in your organization. There is no room in a vibrant society for such nonsense and insensitivity.

We need to acknowledge the importance of our academic institutions by demonstrating our support, interviewing and hiring their graduates, and demanding of our government officials the competitive requirement of having the best college and university system in the world. The best country in the world needs the best academic foundation if it is to remain the best.

To be a successful business leader in tomorrow's time of crisis, you will need to recognize that the new world stretching out in front of us constitutes tremendous opportunities as it seeks our lessons and experiences of democracy and capitalism. Reach out to that world. But there's much more. Don't lose sight of those people, at home and abroad, who need your help. Do what you can to provide them with the opportunities to improve their own lives. Help lift them out of poverty and ignorance and repression by remembering the lessons of that hundred-person world village. And understand that your work, that all of our work, has just begun.

Epilogue

REACH, LIFT,
AND EMBRACE

As I bring this discourse to a close, I can't help but respond to the fear and dismay I see in the eyes of my fellow citizens.

Not a day goes by without my receiving calls from friends, or friends of friends, seeking advice relative to their investments, retirement, or future. Typically they ask if they should get out of the market after already experiencing a 40 percent decline in their portfolios. Their IRAs, their 401(k)s, and any and all investment properties have all precipitously declined in value. Their homes, once valued at perhaps $800,000, now sit next to a foreclosure or alongside a comparable home that recently sold for $550,000.

It is human nature that drives us to think that the portfolio that cost us $500,000, then rose to $1 million, and now has backed down in value to $600,000 is a loss of $400,000 rather than still having a gain of $100,000. The home purchased for $600,000 that rose to $800,000 and has now fallen back down to $550,000 is considered a loss of $250,000, not a loss of $50,000.

Why do we think this way? Partly it is because during the past decade, we experienced only rising tides. Our net worth, our real estate, and our investments went straight up. We experienced a decade of low inflation, increased productivity, and the opening of the global markets. Unprecedented global growth has spoiled us all, or at least spoiled our expectations.

Very smart people, including CEOs, analysts, regulators, and government officials, all got caught up in the euphoria. They fostered and took advantage of cheap money and over-leverage. Today, as we all face the consequences, these same people react by blaming others for the fiasco. The talking heads on television accelerate the fear and fuel the fire by seeking the next target to fuel a yellow journalistic headline that predictably boosts their ratings. Unqualified people take the podium to pontificate their next astute observation of the obvious. None of these reactions, from who did it to whom we should shoot next, are going to alleviate the crisis or instill the confidence that corporate America, consumers, and the markets are desperately seeking. And the reengagement of all three is a prerequisite for a solution.

We have a new president and a new administration with an electoral mandate for change. Their new policies, budgets, and plans, announced on nearly a daily basis, are far from perfect, being perhaps a bit knee jerk in nature. But they do constitute a call to action. Some of the value of these efforts gets diluted by legacy set-asides or shameful pork belly pile-ons. In my opinion, however, we are better off supporting our new president and giving him a chance to rectify the legacy bureaucratic nonsense later, when the current crisis abates, and he can better afford the time and political collateral. I believe that he is responding to the crisis and is exercising the leadership and communication skills that are paramount in restoring confidence.

However, I remain totally disenchanted with our congressional leaders and look to my fellow voters to demand more accountability and transparency from them. If we remove the ideologues and those yet to be weaned from special interest groups, we can return control of our government to the majority. I sense that movement beginning, particularly from our young, newly engaged generation, and I welcome their enthusiasm and involvement.

I predict one of two outcomes from our current economic crisis. The first assumes that corporate America substantially completes the deleveraging required to position themselves in a fashion relative to their current economic realities. I believe that could be achieved by the fourth quarter of 2009, although at the horrific expense of a 10 to 12 percent unemployment rate. This outcome also presumes that the new administration keeps the credit markets liquid and stable (which includes new mark to market rules), that the stimulus package reemploys up to 2 million Americans, and that the remnants of the Troubled Assets Relief Program plan be totally focused on reducing foreclosures and stabilizing real estate values. Policies such as these will stem the economic decline despite two coming waves of stress: deterioration in commercial real estate occupancy rates and valuations and a massive wave of credit card defaults; we have experienced both in previous economic cycles. If all of this happens, both the good and the bad, then in the last quarter of 2009, we will tangibly begin our recovery. We won't return to the growth rates of the past decade, but will experience slow to moderate growth that will be sustainable.

The second outcome assumes that the required policies are not put in place or are not executed properly. In that case, I believe we will be confronting a two- to three-year recession during which unemployment could climb as high as 15 percent. This scenario will create new challenges, particularly for young graduating students and for current and near-term retirees. This will be a very difficult two to three years, but it will not be a repeat of 1931. It will, however, require a shared response by family and friends and from both the haves and the have-nots.

In either outcome, the United States will more than likely emerge as the leader out of the worldwide recession or the nation least effected by it. In essence, in the land of the blind, the one-eyed man is king. Not that any of this should give us solace, but most of the rest of the world has more serious problems than we do. Our recognition of their plight, and our understanding of the interdependencies our economy has with the rest of the world, mandates that we engage in a global solution with the other nations of the world.

How do I answer the multiple inquiries I receive daily? I suggest the following.

One, be supportive of our new president whether you voted for him or not.

Two, support the initiatives that will deliver the first outcome (which I believe is more likely) I outlined earlier.

And three, move cautiously with your investments until there is more clarity as to the direction of the recession, but move nevertheless.

In response to getting out of the market, I believe it is too late; that train has left the station. However, you should change cars on the train. I suggest that if your risk tolerance is at least moderate, you shift to a new 70/30 allocation: 70 percent of your assets should be positioned at one end of the barbell in safe types of instruments, such as cash, cash equivalents, municipal bonds, and a small percentage of high-quality, high-dividend stocks. At the other end of the barbell, you should invest 30 percent in aggressive speculative investments, such as biotech stocks, private equity, and perhaps some bargain real estate buys. Leave nothing in the middle of the barbell, as there is no premium to be gained there. You may miss some moves, but when we recover, you will be in a position to invest a portion of your 70 percent liquid assets with more predictability. And if only a small portion of those speculative investments works, you will do quite well.

We have all experienced weak economic cycles before. Admittedly, in my lifetime, none has been as bad as this one. What I can assure you from the lessons I learned from those weak economies, and from business and physical crises, is that unless you maintain a cool head, a positive attitude, and a willingness to fight disparity, you will surely lose. Don't listen to the doomsday naysayers, because they don't have any of the winning attributes that allow you to confront crisis. Live by the Theodore Roosevelt quote at the start of this book that states the critic doesn't count. We will get through these tough times, and despite the scars we will earn in doing so, it will be worth the legacy we leave our children.

Legacy is in part what led me to write the letter to my son that launched the journey resulting in this book. And it is legacy and my hopes for the next generation that prompt me to accept nearly every invitation I'm extended to speak to young people. At those speeches, there's one theme I always stress, and it's one I'd also like to stress to you, the readers of this book.

In 2006 I agreed to be the commencement speaker for Babson College. At my request, the college sent me some of its promotional materials so I could familiarize myself with its curricula and get a pulse on the student body. One particular brochure exemplified the attitudes of the students. Its cover stated: "I want a college that lives 24/7. I want to be my own boss someday. I want the truth. But most of all I want to stop wanting and start living."

In response to that stated desire, I crafted a speech suggesting that as the graduates evolve, as the realities of work, relationships, family, and citizenship coalesce and segment into defined phases of their lives, they will come to appreciate their consequences. Those phases will produce several defining moments that will influence their lives, dictate their successes as well as their failures, and, most important of all, define their sense of self. I went on to share with them the phases of my life and the corresponding consequences that I experienced.

As I wound up my commencement address and looked at the four hundred students as well as their families and friends, I left them with this theme:

> When you culminate your magnificent achievement
> today by throwing that cap on your head into the sky,
> keep that arm extended throughout your life. Reach
> for the stars, because in our country the stars are
> reachable. With your other arm, reach down and help
> lift those who are less fortunate because they need

your help. Then, with both arms, embrace the United States of America and make it even better through positive reinforcement and constructive criticism. It's all right to be a patriot. Patriots of yesterday, today, and tomorrow protect your rights to graduate. If, for the rest of your life, you apply those simple arm movements I suggest—reach, lift, and embrace—then I promise you what I would wish for you: in that stolen moment one evening, after a hard day's work, when you are washing your face, your reflection in the mirror will get your attention and you will say to yourself, "I made a difference. I like what I see. I have stopped wanting. I am living." God bless you, and God bless America.

As important as this message is to a graduating student body, it is equally important to every business manager. Those simple three words—reach, lift, embrace—can be the catalyst to create a healthy, positive attitude; they can shape your humanity and discipline your hierarchy; and they can commit you to establishing an even greater legacy for your children. If you can put this book down having gained the insight of those three words, then I will have achieved what I set out to do: make you the best leader you can be.

Thank you for your time and attention,

Joe Grano

ABOUT THE AUTHORS

Joseph J. Grano Jr. is chairman and CEO of Centurion Holdings LLC, a company that advises private and public companies.

Previously Grano served as chairman of UBS Financial Services (formerly UBS PaineWebber). He oversaw a series of dramatic events at the firm, including its merger with UBS and its response to the attacks of September 11, 2001. In 2002 he was appointed by President George W. Bush to serve as chairman of the Homeland Security Advisory Council. Prior to joining PaineWebber, Grano was with Merrill Lynch for sixteen years, rising from stockbroker trainee to director of national sales. He was chairman of the Board of Governors of the NASD and a member of the NASD's Executive Committee.

Before joining Merrill Lynch, Grano served in the U.S. Army. He became one of the army's youngest officers, achieving the rank of captain. He commanded a Special Forces (Green Berets) A Team in Latin America and an infantry company in Vietnam. Severely wounded in combat, he was awarded the Bronze Star with V device for valor.

Grano holds honorary doctor of law degrees from Pepperdine University and Babson College, honorary doctor of humane letters degrees from Queens College, City University of New York, and Central Connecticut State University, and an honorary doctor of business administration degree from the University of New Haven.

Grano has received the Corporate Leadership Award from the Thurgood Marshall Scholarship Fund, the USO Gold Medal Award for Distinguished Service, the Business Leader of the Year award from Georgetown University's School of Business, the La Bellissima America award from the Italian American Museum, and the Ellis Island Medal of Honor. He has also won a Tony Award as a producer of the record-setting musical *Jersey Boys*.

Mark Levine has written and collaborated on more than thirty books, including the best sellers *Second Acts, Die Broke,* and *Lifescripts*. He has been a contributing editor to *Worth* and a columnist for *Men's Health* and *Working Woman*. He is the author of hundreds of magazine articles, three of which were nominated for the American Society of Magazine Editors' National Magazine Awards. Levine has taught magazine writing at Cornell University and has been a guest lecturer at Syracuse University's Newhouse School of Journalism. He is a member of the Authors Guild.

ACKNOWLEDGMENTS

There are hundreds of people who deserve acknowledgment for the support they've given me throughout my life and career and, most recently, in the writing of this book. There are superiors who taught me, encouraged me, and watched my back. There are peers who worked with me, laughed with me, and kept me centered. And there are subordinates who bled for me and worked for me, and whose loyalty and efforts inspired me. But in order to keep these acknowledgments to a reasonable length, I'll focus on the contributions of my direct reports.

Thanks to Mark Sutton, Robert Silver, Margo Alexander, Regina Dolan, James MacGilvray, Theodore Levine, Michael Culp, Steve Baum, Brian Barefoot, Robert Pangia, Michael Madden, and Concetta Kristan. Thank you to Karen Murphy and the team at Jossey-Bass for their guidance and assistance. And special thanks to Mark Levine for his friendship, collaboration, and for being the "rudder in my chaotic sea."

INDEX